Cambridge Elements

Elements in Rethinking Byzantium
edited by
Leonora Neville
University of Wisconsin Madison
Darlene Brooks Hedstrom
Brandeis University

KYIVAN RUS IN MEDIEVAL EUROPE

Christian Raffensperger
Wittenberg University

Shaftesbury Road, Cambridge CB2 8EA, United Kingdom

One Liberty Plaza, 20th Floor, New York, NY 10006, USA

477 Williamstown Road, Port Melbourne, VIC 3207, Australia

314–321, 3rd Floor, Plot 3, Splendor Forum, Jasola District Centre, New Delhi – 110025, India

103 Penang Road, #05–06/07, Visioncrest Commercial, Singapore 238467

Cambridge University Press is part of Cambridge University Press & Assessment, a department of the University of Cambridge.

We share the University's mission to contribute to society through the pursuit of education, learning and research at the highest international levels of excellence.

www.cambridge.org
Information on this title: www.cambridge.org/9781009570015

DOI: 10.1017/9781009570022

When citing this work, please include a reference to the DOI 10.1017/9781009570022

First published 2025

A catalogue record for this publication is available from the British Library

ISBN 978-1-009-57001-5 Hardback
ISBN 978-1-009-57004-6 Paperback
ISSN 3033-4292 (online)
ISSN 3033-4284 (print)

Additional resources for this publication at www.cambridge.org/raffensperger

Kyivan Rus in Medieval Europe

Elements in Rethinking Byzantium

DOI: 10.1017/9781009570022
First published online: February 2025

Christian Raffensperger
Wittenberg University

Author for correspondence: Christian Raffensperger, craffensperger@wittenberg.edu

Abstract: While there has been a great deal (comparatively) written about Rus as part of medieval Europe in the last twenty years, the popular perception of it remains a part of the so-called "Byzantine Commonwealth." This traditional framing discounts Rusian ties to the west and exaggerates those to "Byzantium," elevating the rhetoric used by Russian nationalists to separate Russia from Europe. This Element provides an accurate historical account of medieval Rus that corrects the modern misuse of medieval history: a resource for academics interested in the results of current research on the place of the Kingdom of Rus in the medieval world. It brings together and synthesizes existing scholarship on Rus to present a complete picture of the kingdom of Rus, and its orientation within the wider medieval world, with a particular focus on the eleventh and twelfth centuries.

Keywords: Rus, medieval Europe, Byzantium, medieval politics, Slavic Europe

ISBNs: 9781009570015 (HB), 9781009570046 (PB), 9781009570022 (OC)
ISSNs: 3033-4292 (online), 3033–4284 (print)

Contents

Introduction: Rus, Russia, Ukraine

Numerous scholars have now made the case that the Enlightenment period helped to shape our modern perception of the past. Whether this was Anthony Kaldellis talking about the creation of "Byzantium" or Larry Wolff discussing the *Invention of Eastern Europe*, one can turn to good scholarship to understand what happened 300 years ago and its effects on our understanding of history.[1] What is missing though is our integration of that material into our modern understanding of why that matters. The case of medieval Rus and modern Ukraine is an excellent one to use to explore what happened to create a separate medieval East and West and why that matters in the present.

A year before Russian President Vladimir Putin's 2022 full-scale invasion of Ukraine, he published a piece entitled "On the Historical Unity of Russians and Ukrainians."[2] In that article Putin repeated the long-standing belief that Russians were Great Russians and Ukrainians were simply Little Russians. To do this, he used history as his guide. He did not just go back to the seventeenth century when Tsar Aleksei Mikhailovich was the first to use the title "Sovereign of Great, Little, and White Russia." Instead, he went all the way back to the Middle Ages and the medieval kingdom of Rus to demonstrate that the Ukrainians and Russians were the same people. In particular, he quoted the *Povest' vremennykh let* (often translated as the Tale of Bygone Years), the earliest Rusian source, to say, "Let [Kiev] be the mother of all Russian cities."[3] Which is not that different from the only English translation of that source: Oleg "declared that [Kiev] should be the mother of Russian cities."[4] This translation, published in 1953 but prepared earlier, is titled *The Russian Primary Chronicle*. And here we can see elements of the problem quite clearly. Both Vladimir Putin and the translator of the chronicle are stating that the history of the ninth-century polity and the early twelfth-century source are all Russian. Such a label makes it much easier to elide the medieval kingdom of Rus into the modern country of Russia and erase anyone else's claim to the medieval past of that region. A more accurate translation of the same phrase from the chronicle would be, "Let this

---

[1] Anthony Kaldellis, *Romanland: Ethnicity and Empire in Byzantium* (Cambridge, MA: Harvard University Press, 2019); Larry Wolff, *Inventing Eastern Europe: The Map of Civilization on the Mind of the Enlightenment* (Stanford: Stanford University Press, 1994).

[2] http://en.kremlin.ru/events/president/news/66181.

[3] The best edition of the PVL, as it is known, is *The Povest' vremennykh let: An Interlinear Collation and Paradosis*, Compiled and edited by Donald Ostrowski, with David Birnbaum and Horace G. Lunt (Cambridge, MA: Harvard University Press, 2004).

[4] *The Russian Primary Chronicle: Laurentian Text*, transl. and ed. Samuel Hazzard Cross and Olgerd P. Sherbowitz-Wetzor (Cambridge, MA: The Mediaeval Academy of America, 1953), s.a. 882.

[Kyiv] be the mother of the towns of Rus'."[5] Taking away the idea that medieval Rus was Russia is one step, but a large one, in attempting to shift our perception of medieval and modern Europe.

However, it is worth examining how medieval Europe became so divided, and why, to help us better understand and move away from those perspectives. As noted earlier, the Enlightenment played a key role, especially in regard to Orthodoxy. Orthodox Christianity was viewed as even more outdated, old, and traditional than Catholicism, which was more common in the lives of the Enlightenment thinkers. Many have traced the anti-religious streak back to Edward Gibbon's *Decline and Fall of the Roman Empire*, with John Arnold stating, "Gibbon has bequeathed to us a particular way of looking at religious credulity as the opposite of Reason and thus as a threat to civilization, a view which tends to recur in current debate."[6] Gibbon's later eighteenth-century writings did not appear in a vacuum and is contextualized with numerous instances where Orthodoxy was treated as not just the enemy of Reason, but of the Western order, as well. In the sixteenth and seventeenth centuries, broad sheets published in German cities told about the atrocities of the Russians using identical language – in fact the broadsheets were the same, with only the perpetrators replaced – as when they discussed the Ottoman Turks.[7] Similarly, after Peter the Great's victory at Poltava in 1709, an official of King George I stated that "Germany and the entire North have never been in such grave peril as now, because the Russians should be feared more than the Turks . . . and are gradually advancing closer and closer to our lives."[8] Long gone were the days of any Christian unity, in its place was an identification by Western Europeans that Orthodoxy was as much of a threat, if not more, than the dominant Islamic empire in Western Afro-Eurasia.

Even if we advance to the twentieth century, the division of Europe with Orthodoxy at its heart is not just still present but increasingly codified. J. B. Bury, not coincidentally a scholar of Gibbon, divided his massive *Cambridge Medieval History* project such that eastern Europe was allocated into one volume. He explained his rationale quite clearly in his introduction:

[5] Here I have followed the draft version of the translation which will be published by the Harvard Ukrainian Research Institute.

[6] John Arnold, "Believing in Belief: Gibbon, Latour and the Social History of Religion," *Past & Present* 260 (2023), 241.

[7] Cornelia Soldat, *Erschreckende Geschichten in der Darstellung von Moskovitern und Osmanen in den deutschen Flugschriften des 16. und 17. Jahrhunderts / Stories of Atrocities in Sixteenth and Seventeenth Century German Pamphlets about the Russians and Turks* (Lewiston: Edwin Mellen Press, 2014).

[8] Quoted in Lindsay Hughes, "Russia," in *A Companion to Eighteenth-Century Europe*, ed. Peter H. Wilson (New York: Blackwell, 2008), 239.

> This exception to the general chronological plan of the world seemed both convenient and desirable. The orbit of Byzantium, the history of the peoples and states which moved within that orbit and always looked to it as the central body, giver of light and heat, did indeed at some points touch or traverse the orbits of western European states, but the development of these on the whole was not deeply affected or sensibly perturbed by what happened east of Italy or south of the Danube, and it was only in the time of the Crusades that some of their rulers came into close contact with the Eastern Empire or that it counted to any considerable extent in their policies.[9]

For Bury, Europe may exist as a geographic entity, but medieval Europe largely refers to western Europe and eastern Europe is relegated to a Byzantine sphere of influence. Dimitri Obolensky took this a step further when, in the 1970s, he codified the idea of a *Byzantine Commonwealth*.[10] The organizing principle of Obolensky's commonwealth was the tacit acknowledgment of the Byzantine emperor's authority over the whole of Orthodox Christendom. Thus, he does not include such areas of Byzantine influence as Venice, Sicily, or the Caucasus; because they do not fit into the Orthodox-centered scheme which he has created. Garth Fowden, who took classes with Obolensky at Oxford, makes this quite clear when he notes that Obolensky's commonwealth constituted, "the Chalcedonian Orthodox world of Slavic Eastern Europe."[11] A combination of the foregoing ideas has led us to the modern world of medieval studies where there exists a "medieval Europe" which comprises largely western Europe, though Iberia, Scandinavia, and Central Europe are making inroads into this territory; and a Byzantine world which includes the Orthodox Balkans and Rus. Whether one looks in textbooks, job ads, or conference programs, one can see this pattern replicated.

But how then does this relate to Rus, Ukraine, and Russia? The Russian narrative of history was codified by Vasilii Kliuchevsky in the late nineteenth and early twentieth centuries in his famous *History of Russia*. These books inspired a generation of historians and Kliuchevsky himself was, in the words of his biographer, "Russia's most distinguished historian and whose teaching, writing and training of young scholars have markedly affected the way Russians and others view Russia's past."[12] Kliuchevsky's *History of Russia*

---

[9] J. B. Bury, "Introduction," *The Cambridge Medieval History* vol. IV *The Eastern Roman Empire (717-1453)* (New York: The MacMillan Company, 1923), vii.

[10] Dimitri Obolensky, *The Byzantine Commonwealth, Eastern Europe 500–1453* (London: Weidenfeld and Nicolson, 1971).

[11] Garth Fowden, *Empire to Commonwealth: Consequences of Monotheism in Late Antiquity* (Princeton: Princeton University Press, 1993), 9–10. See also 4n3 where he says that "My indebtedness to Obolensky will be self-evident. His book appeared in 1971, just when, as a first-year undergraduate at Oxford, I was attending his remarkable lectures on Byzantine historical geography."

[12] Robert F. Byrnes, *V. O. Kliuchevskii, Historian of Russia* (Bloomington: Indiana University Press, 1995), xvii. Further, Byrnes notes that "His five-volume *Course of Russian History* . . .

was translated into eleven languages, including English, and his students taught Russian history across Europe and in North America, thus his ideas spread widely. His view on Rus was that it was simply Russia and in his volume 1, the material is largely related to Rusian–Byzantine ties.[13] There are no mentions of the manifold dynastic marriages which connected Rus throughout Europe in this period, nor the breadth of religious and trade relations. When non-Rusian or Byzantine influences are included, they are negative. In fighting against the "barbarians of the steppe" Rus held "the left flank of Europe. Yet this historical service cost her dear, since not only did it dislodge her from her old settlements on the Dnieper, but it caused the whole trend of her life to become altered."[14] In addition to a lack of Rus, there is also a lack of Rusians in his narrative. "He ignored the existence of separate Ukrainian and Belorussian nationalities and cultures and those who proclaimed it: in his judgment, these peoples were Russians."[15] Moreover, in later volumes, he dealt with the Russian conquest of the lands of Ukrainians and Belorussians as a historical inevitability akin to manifest destiny, often under the label of the "gathering of the Rus lands." His views codified the belief of a Russian world that comprised eastern Europe and was connected to, if not descended from, the Byzantine Orthodox world; and created the basis for this to be taught and perpetuated until the present day.[16]

Kliuchevsky's narrative has been called the "traditional scheme of Russian history," and this is accurate, but not inclusive.[17] Due to the popularity of the "traditional scheme," Russian history writ large – which is to say eastern European history or Orthodox European history – became its own field and thus could be safely excluded from other regions, such as medieval European history. A cursory glance at a popular medieval Europe textbook will show the place of Rus, and other Orthodox polities:

> "The 'border' that divides Catholic from Orthodox in the Balkans is today roughly the border between Croatia (Catholic) and Serbia (Orthodox). When we think about the wars in the Balkans that occurred in the 1990s, it is important to remember that many of the divisions are at least in part along religious lines – Catholics, Orthodox, and Muslims (remember that Ottoman

---

which is almost certainly the most widely read and influential study of Russian history ever published."

13 V. O. Kliuchevsky, *A History of Russia*, Vol. 1, transl. C. J. Hogarth (New York: Russell and Russell, 1960), 79–85.

14 Kliuchevsky, *A History of Russia*, Vol. 1, 192–193.

15 Byrnes, *V. O. Kliuchevskii*, 145–146.

16 Not to say that Kliuchevsky did not have opponents. The most famous of whom was his contemporary Mykhailo Hrushevsky who wrote a multivolume *History of Ukraine-Rus'* in which Rus is deeply integrated into medieval history. This series has recently been translated in full into English by the Canadian Institute of Ukrainian Studies.

17 Serhii Plokhy, *Unmaking Imperial Russia: Mykhailo Hrushevsky and the Writing of Ukrainian History* (Toronto: University of Toronto Press, 2005), 146.

> Turks ruled the southern Balkans for more than four hundred years beginning in the last century of the Byzantine Empire) – that were first established during the Middle Ages."[18]
>
> "Like the Balkan Slavs, the Russians received their religion and much of their culture from Constantinople. Indeed, after the fall of Constantinople to the Ottoman Turks in 1453, the Russians began to think of themselves as heirs to the Roman Empire: just as Rome had given way to Constantinople, so now has the torch passed to the third and final Rome, Moscow"[19]

To conclude their narrative, the authors make clear their perspective on the division in Europe and its consequences by suggesting that "When we think of problems and misunderstandings within Europe today, we in large part think of tensions and conflicts that exist along the lines of Western and Byzantine spheres of influence, for example, the line between Poland and Russia or that between Croatia and Serbia."[20] For these authors, as well as for many authors not cited here, the division between Latin and Orthodox in the middle ages are replicated in the problems of the modern world.

A division in Europe based on historical and religious divisions can be seen in current political issues. The United Nations definition of the term "Eastern Europe" exemplifies the issues under discussion: "that part of the European continent that has been 'under Byzantine and Orthodox influence, which has only randomly been touched by an Ottoman impact, but significantly shaped by Russian influence during the Russian Empire and in the Soviet period'."[21] The eastern part of Europe is no longer just a geographical definition, but a categorical one which is based, in large part, around Orthodoxy. The North Atlantic Treaty Organization (NATO) was created in the wake of World War II, and its mission was to oppose the Soviet Union and its expansion. Yet, the first NATO Secretary General, Lord Ismay, colloquially stated the organization's purpose as "to keep the Russians out, the Americans in, and the Germans down."[22] Apart from the fascinating comments about Americans and Germans, the focus for Lord Ismay was not the Soviet Union, but Russia and the Russians – perhaps creating a link with the quote from the official of George

[18] William R. Cook and Ronald B. Herzman, *The Medieval World View: An Introduction* (Oxford: Oxford University Press [3rd ed.], 2012), 104–105.

[19] Cook and Herzman, *The Medieval World View*, 105.

[20] Cook and Herzman, *The Medieval World View*, 114.

[21] Florin Curta, *Eastern Europe in the Middle Ages (500–1300)* (Leiden: Brill, 2019), vol. 1, 4. The internal citation is to Peter Jordan, "A Subdivision of Europe into Larger Regions by Cultural Criteria," United Nations Group of Experts on Geographical Names, Working Paper no. 48, 23rd session, Vienna, March 28–April 4, 2006, http://unstats.un.org/unsd/geoinfo/UNGEGN/docs/23-gegn/wp/gegn23wp48.pdf (visit of September 25, 2018).

[22] Quoted in Fyodor Lukyanov, "Transatlantic Transformation: U.S.-German Relations Enter New Era," *Carnegie Russia Eurasia Center*, published June 29, 2020.

I two hundred years earlier. Lord Ismay's interpretation of the organization's mission was implicitly ratified in the years after 1991 when the fall of the Soviet Union did not mean the disbanding of NATO; instead, it expanded. The expansion of NATO brought it closer and closer to the Russian border, despite multiple warnings from Boris Yeltsin, Putin, and various Russia experts that this was seen as threatening.

We could take our argument one step further and unite the themes of Orthodoxy and European identity. The European Union (EU) comprises twenty-seven member states, of which three are majority Orthodox countries (Bulgaria, Greece, and Romania). The other majority Orthodox countries in Europe are Belarus, Moldova, North Macedonia, Russia, Serbia, and Ukraine.

As can be seen in Figure 1, the Orthodox countries comprise the majority of Europe which is not included in the EU. If one includes the European Economic Area (which adds numerous western and northern European countries), one can see the outliers are all Orthodox countries. Thus, the logical conclusion is that the territory of the European continent which we traditionally label "Europe" is largely non-Orthodox, while the rest, which is typically labeled "Eastern

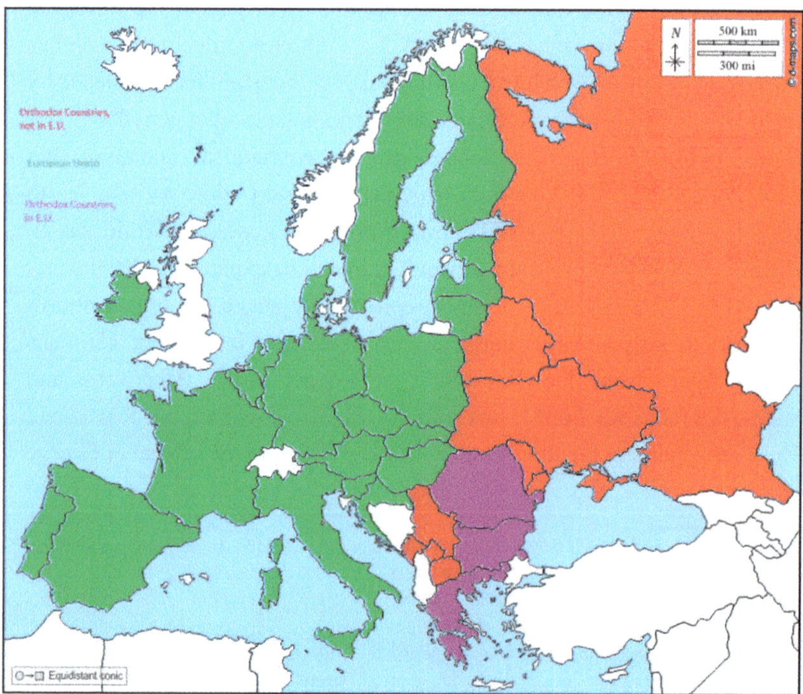

Figure 1 Map of Europe designating Orthodox countries not in the EU (red), the European Union (green), and the Orthodox countries in the EU (purple). (This figure is also available to view online in colour at www.cambridge.org/raffensperger)

Europe" is Orthodox; creating a frame which has caused problems for Ukraine's ability to join the EU, among many other issues.

Education is a blessing, but an incorrect understanding of history can create problems. Medieval history matters for so many reasons, but one is that it sets expectations for modern perceptions. A medieval Europe that is inclusive of Rus and thus stretches from the Ural Mountains to the Atlantic Ocean will help to shift our perception of Europe not only in that period, but in our own.

The sections in this slim volume will attempt to do a broad task, elucidate the history of the kingdom of Rus and its relationship with the rest of Europe. Section 1: "Situating Rus" is intended as a brief introduction to the foundation of the kingdom, some of its early actors and its relationship to the world around it, both in history and in historiography. Section 2 is on religion and thus tackles the issue highlighted in the Introduction, the conversion of Rus to Christianity. Instead of a traditional picture of Orthodox dominance, this section will highlight the position of Rus within the broader Christian world. Section 3 examines the kingdom of Rus itself with a specific focus on governance, both top down and local. This is an important topic in the historiography because Rus's decentralized government has often led to perceptions of them as an "other." Section 4 brings the world back in and discusses the place of Rus in Europe. Far from the traditional "Route from the Varangians to the Greeks," Rus was tied in to most corners of Europe through dynastic and other relations. The sum total of this short overview of Kyivan Rus in Medieval Europe will demonstrate the importance of accurate representations of history, both for its own sake, as well as for our understanding of the world around us.

1 Situating Rus

Rus seldom appears on modern maps of medieval Europe. Instead, if the map is comprehensive, it may use "Russia" to label that part of the eastern Europe; while if the map is not, it will most likely leave the area blank, or occlude it behind the key explaining what is going on in Western Europe. Regardless of the historiographical issues embedded here, we need to begin with setting the stage for where Rus was, what it was, and how we know anything about it before we can properly contextualize it in regard to medieval Europe as a whole.

The kingdom of Rus was founded by Scandinavians who explored the eastern European river systems. Unlike expansion westward from Norway, which is often described as requiring the dual advances of keel and sail; going east around the Baltic was a much simpler task which could be, and was, accomplished by oared boats.[23]

[23] For an excellent, and overarching, discussion of how the Scandinavian exploration west and east were different, see Thomas S. Noonan, "Scandinavians in European Russia," in *The Oxford Illustrated History of the Vikings*, ed. Peter Sawyer (Oxford: Oxford University Press, 1997), 134–155.

Evidence for amber and fur trade, and as loot from raids, comes from an earlier period than what we see for the start of the Viking age. The traditional, and still dominant, explanation for the expansion of Scandinavians into eastern Europe is focused on the acquisition of silver. There were no native silver deposits in Scandinavia or in northeastern Europe, but by the later eighth century, silver began appearing in the Baltic. The source of silver were dirhams, Islamic coins from the Abbasid Caliphate. Those coins made their way up the Volga River via trade with the Khazars, Bulgars, and local Slavic and Finnic populations. Thomas Noonan, who studied the numismatics of Rus extensively, suggests that 36 percent of the silver coming into eastern Europe in the period 780–830 was exported to the Baltic.[24] This amount increased each decade subsequently and in the early ninth century finds begin to appear along the Dnieper River route as well, largely on the left bank (eastern side) of the river. Noonan concludes that "once it became known that Ladoga [a town in the north on Lake Ladoga] was the chief outlet for the export of Islamic dirhams to the eastern Baltic, peoples from all over the Baltic came to Ladoga to obtain these coins."[25] One can see the impact of that silver in the rise of Birka and Gotland in the ninth century.[26] In addition to silver, eastern Europe was a source for other goods such as the aforementioned amber and furs, as well as slaves.[27]

Scandinavians came into eastern Europe searching for these goods, but they also made a life there. In the earliest excavated settlement layer from Ladoga, dated 750–830, numerous goods with ties to Scandinavia have been found, including Frisian style bone combs, wooden toy swords of Frankish style, and leather shoes which can be found around the rim of the Baltic as in Norway.[28] Even farther afield, near Lake Kubenskoye (700 kilometers to the east of Ladoga) tenth-century finds of glass beads are similar to what is found in Birka, in both style and quantity.[29] In fact, Ingmar Jansson notes that "Mainland Scandinavian artefacts are abundant, found in settlements, graves and hoards throughout the land of Rus – in political and economic centres and also in some rural regions."[30]

---

24 Thomas S. Noonan, "Why the Vikings First Came to Russia," in *The Islamic World, Russia and the Vikings, 750–900: The Numismatic Evidence* (Brookfield: Ashgate, 1998), 343–344.

25 Noonan, "Why the Vikings First Came to Russia," 345.

26 Dan Carlsson, "Gotland: Silver Island," in *Viking-Age Trade: Silver, Slaves and Gotland*, ed. Jacek Gruszczyński, Marek Jankowiak and Jonathan Shepard (New York: Routledge, 2022): 225–241.

27 Janet Martin, *Treasure of the Land of Darkness: The Fur Trade and its Significance for Medieval Russia* (Cambridge: Cambridge University Press, 1986).

28 Noonan, "Why the Vikings First Came to Russia," 332–335.

29 N. Makarov. "Traders in the Forest: The Northern Periphery of Rus' in the Medieval Trade Network," in *Pre-Modern Russia and Its World: Essays in Honor of Thomas S. Noonan*, ed. Kathryn L. Reyerson, Theofanis G. Stavrou, James D. Tracy (Wiesbaden: Harrassowitz, 2006), 121–123.

30 Ingmar Jansson, "Gotland Viewed from the Swedish Mainland," in *Viking-Age Trade: Silver, Slaves and Gotland*, ed. Jacek Gruszczyński, Marek Jankowiak and Jonathan Shepard (New York: Routledge, 2022), 336.

All of which creates a solid basis for the interactions between Scandinavians and eastern Europeans in the material record.

Textual sources for the Scandinavian presence along the eastern European river systems are more complicated. Viking raids on Anglo-Saxon England, Ireland, and the Carolingian territories are all well recorded by contemporaries, or those writing slightly later. This profusion of sources is due to a literate populace being raided, often monks in monasteries, as well as the widespread network generated by the Northumbrian renaissance. Eastern Europe was not Christianized, and thus, we have no monasteries to raid or monks to write about such raids. For early textual sources we must rely on those preserved in Arabic and Greek, as the Scandinavians reached the Caspian and Black Sea regions, and a few in Latin typically about trade. The Arabic sources provide us with the earliest textual glimpse of Rus. Ibn Khurradādhbih was the director of the Abbasid intelligence service in the late ninth and early tenth centuries. In the middle of the ninth century, he wrote a report about the Radhanite merchants traveling through eastern Europe and into Abbasid territory. Within that report is a section on Rusian merchants. He describes them as "one of the Saqaliba people" which is a word typically used for Slavs, and they are from the farthest reaches of that land, implying the north.[31] Early in the next century, Mas'ūdī says that "the Rūs are many nations, divided into different groups."[32] And then relates that they travel "far and wide, trading with al-Andalus, Rome, Constantinople and the Khazars." Relations with the Khazars, a raid upon whom Mas'ūdī records, also provide an entry point for Arabic sources on Rus. Istakhrī, writing in the mid-tenth century, suggests that "there are three sorts of Rūs. One sort lives near Bulghār and their king dwells in a city called Kiev; it is larger than Bulghār. Another sort live further away; they are called Slovenes [Salāwīya]. And there is a sort called Arthānīya; their king lives in Arthā and the people come to trade in Kiev."[33] Trading, especially along the river systems, is highlighted by Istakhri, especially in sable pelts.

Greek sources also begin in the mid-ninth century with a report by Patriarch Photius regarding an attack on Constantinople by a "Scythian tribe," "An obscure nation, a nation of no account, a nation ranked among slaves . . . "[34] Scythian is

[31] "Ibn Khurradādhbih on the routes of the Rādhānīya and the Rūs c. 830," in *Ibn Fadlan and the Land of Darkness: Arab Travellers in the Far North*, transl. Paul Lunde and Caroline Stone (New York: Penguin, 2012), 112.

[32] "Mas'ūdī on a Viking Raid on the Casptian, c. 913," in *Ibn Fadlan and the Land of Darkness: Arab Travellers in the Far North*, transl. Paul Lunde and Caroline Stone (New York: Penguin, 2012), 144.

[33] "Istakhrī on the Khazars and their neighbours, c. 951," in *Ibn Fadlan and the Land of Darkness: Arab Travellers in the Far North*, transl. Paul Lunde and Caroline Stone (New York: Penguin, 2012), 158.

[34] Cyril Mango, *The Homilies of Photius Patriarch of Constantinople* (Cambridge, MA: Harvard University Press, 1958), 89, 98.

a generic term used in the medieval Roman Empire to describe those to their north, across the Black Sea. Photius does refer to "*Rhos*" in the titles of his homilies (III and IV), but not in the text. Later in the 860s he uses "*Rhos*" in an encyclical to the other patriarchs, telling of a mission to convert them, and referencing the 860 attack on Constantinople.[35] This same information is included in the text of Theophanes Continuatus, who wrote in the middle of the tenth century, possibly under the sponsorship of Emperor Constantine VII *Porphyrogenitos*.[36] It is also included in John Skylitzes, writing in the eleventh century.[37] The possibility of a ninth-century conversion of Rus has been speculated upon by modern authors, but it is difficult given the lack of other sources and the possibility of a repetition of information in three Greek sources.[38] In the tenth century, Rus and its rulers come more into the view of the medieval Romans. In 967, Emperor Nikephoras II Phokas requested assistance from Sviatoslav, the ruler of Rus, against the Bulgars.[39] Both Leo the Deacon and Skylitzes record the various battles of this campaign and have a good deal of information about Sviatoslav and the Rusians who are referred to as Rhos, Scythians, Taurians, and Tauroscythians.

The Latin sources are thin for this early period of the history of Rus. In the early tenth century, the Byzantine emperor Theophilos sent a group of "*Rhos*" to Louis the Pious because they could not return home the way they arrived.[40] After an investigation, Louis the Pious pronounced them to be Swedes, a group which he knew quite well from dealing with Scandinavian raids, and the presence of Danes at his court, such as Harald Klak. According to a new reading by Ildar Garipzanov, it is also possible that they named their ruler as Hakon, a decidedly Scandinavian name.[41] Latin sources also record the presence of the Rusians as traders, akin to what the Arabic sources record. The Raffelstettin regulations of the early tenth century mark the presence of Rusians in the middle

---

35 *Photii patriarchae Constantinopolitani epistulae et amphilochia*, ed. Laourdas, Vasileios and Leendert Gerrit Westerink (Leipzig: BSB B. G. Teubner Verlagsgesellschaft, 1983), vol. 1. 50.

36 Theophanes Continuatus, *Chronographiae quae Theophanis Continuati nomine fertur Libri I-IV*, ed. Jeffrey Michael Featherstone and Juan Signes-Codoñer (Berlin: De Gruyter, 2015), IV.33.

37 John Skylitzes, *A Synopsis of Byzantine History, 811–1057*, transl. John Wortley (Cambridge: Cambridge University Press, 2010), ch. 5, 18. Pp. 107-8; ch. 6, 42. P. 159

38 K. Ericsson. "The Earliest Conversion of the Rus' to Christianity," *Slavonic and East European Review* 44:102 (1966): 98–121.

39 Skylitzes, *A Synopsis of Byzantine History*, ch. 14, sec. 20, p. 265. Leo the Deacon, *The History of Leo the Deacon: Byzantine Military Expansion in the Tenth Century*, transl. Alice-Mary Talbot and Denis F. Sullivan (Washington, DC: Dumbarton Oaks Research Library and Collection, 2005), bk. IV, ch. 6.

40 *The Annals of St-Bertin*, transl. Janet L. Nelson (New York: Manchester University Press, 1991), s.a. 839.

41 Ildar Garipzanov, "The Annals of St. Bertin (839) and *Chacanus* of the *Rhos*," *Ruthenica* 5:1 (2006): 7–11.

Danube region.[42] Largely they traded wax, horses, and slaves and continued to be present in other early tenth-century trading regulations, increasing their identification as traders on an east-west route, not just a north-south one.

Local sources come into the picture rather late. The earliest chronicle source produced in Rus dates to the end of the eleventh and early twelfth centuries. It is known as the *Povest' vremennykh let* (PVL), after its opening phrase. This chronicle begins with the biblical flood, proceeds to the foundation myth for Rus in the ninth century, and then entries become more common in the second half of the tenth century. One quite interesting aspect of this source is the likely interpolation of two treaties between Rus and the Roman Empire, each of which followed raids on Constantinople.[43] The treaties are formulaic in organization, but include specifics on the Rusians, their gods, and their names, indicating a good knowledge between the two groups and possibly providing another early source for Rus.

Having established the early source base for Rus, we can say comfortably that the Rusians were Scandinavians who explored the eastern European river systems and occupied existing towns, dominating local populations, and trading with the Khazars, Bulgars, Romans, Germans, and others. But where do we get this name of Rus? The traditional explanation is based around translation and transmission. The local Finnic speakers on the Baltic coast referred to those coming from Scandinavia as "rowers" (*ruotsi*); as noted earlier, they did not need the advancement of sails to reach the eastern Baltic. When those Finns guided (willingly or otherwise) the Scandinavians into the interior they called them not Scandinavians, Swedes, or any other ethnonym, instead using their own name for them – ruotsi. The Slavs dropped the "ts" into a simple "s" and called those who came "*rusi*." Over time, the ending became softened and is now indicated by a soft sign (rendered in English by a ′), thus Rus′. Though for ease of use, I have excluded the prime and simply use Rus for the place and Rusian for the people throughout.

Normanist Controversy

The beginning of the previous paragraph elides the fact that some scholars do not, in fact, agree that the Rusians were Scandinavians. The controversy between those who do and those who do not believe this has come to be called the "Normanist Controversy," as in were the Rusians Scandinavians (Northmen,

[42] "Mercandi Causa," *Monumenta Germaniae Historica: Capitularia regum Francorum*, ed. Victor Krause, vol. 2 (Hanover: Impensis Bibliopolii, 1897), 251.

[43] PVL, s.a. 912, 945. An account of the latter raid is also recorded in Skylitzes, *A Synopsis of Byzantine History*, ch. 10, sec. 31. P. 221.

Normans)? A brief overview of the controversy is essential to contextualize the history and historiography of Rus.

The 862 entry in the PVL states that the Slavs, having "driven the Varangians overseas," then invited them back in because they could not rule themselves.[44] Accordingly, they sent to the Rusians for a leader. As for who the Rusians were, the chronicler takes pains to point that out, saying, "For that's the way these Varangians called themselves, Rusians: as now others are called Swedes, and others Normans, Angles, still others Goths . . . ." The chronicler is situating the Rusians "overseas" among other Scandinavian peoples such as the Swedes. Similarly, the two treaties interpolated into the PVL between Rus and the medieval Roman Empire includes the signatories; for the 912 treaty, following the imperial names it says, "we of the Rusian nation, Karl, Ingjald, Farulf, Vermund . . . " and so on.[45] The names are almost entirely Scandinavian and they identify themselves as Rusian, solidifying that link. Outside of Rus, we see a similar situation in the Annals of St. Bertin where envoys from Rus come to the court of Louis the Pious and he identified them as Swedes, further linking Rusians and Scandinavians.[46] The case in primary sources seems clear.

In the eighteenth century, however, Mikhail Lomonosov, one of the earliest Russian, rather than German, scholars in the Russian Academy posited a new theory, one grounded in politics. His suggestion was that the Rusians were autochthonous Slavs who were from the Ros River region.[47] The idea that the Rusians were Slavs rather than Swedes was incredibly important in the context of contemporary politics as Peter the Great had recently fought the Swedes for twenty years in the Great Northern War, and they had been a primary rival for more than a century prior. Russia's attempts to link itself to the Kyivan Rus past meant that the foundations of Rus needed to be the foundations of Russia. Thus, if the Slavs could not govern themselves and had to invite in Scandinavians to rule over them, as the PVL states in 862, the contemporary ramifications were a negative portrayal vis-à-vis the ongoing conflict with the Swedes and in regard to the ability of Russia to stand alone as an empire in Europe. Lomonosov's ideas birthed the Normanist controversy. The Normanist position has been consistent and has been stated here. The anti-Normanist position begun by Lomonosov has changed numerous times over the last two hundred years, as various ideas were disproven by textual or archaeological evidence. The persistence of the anti-Normanist position is largely linked to government sponsorship under Imperial, Soviet, and modern Russian regimes which aim to

[44] PVL, s.a. 862. [45] PVL, s.a. 912. [46] *The Annals of St-Bertin*, 44.

[47] M. Lomonosov, *Drevniaia Rossiiskaia istoriia ot nachala rossiiskogo naroda do konchiny velikogo kniazia Iaroslava Pervogo ili do 1054 goda* (St. Petersburg, 1766).

strengthen their idea of nation via an articulation of an independent past.[48] The past, as we should know, is not only another country, but does not exist to validate or legitimize modern polities or their dictators. That the Rusians were Scandinavians is evident in the extant sources and should be able to be discussed without political interference.

A Kyivan Kingdom

The semi-mythical Riurik was succeeded by Oleg, Helgi in the original Scandinavian. The PVL is clear that Oleg belonged to Riurik's family, but Riurik also entrusted his son Igor (Ingvar) to him as well, "as he was very young."[49] Oleg and Igor are historical characters who appear in sources beyond the PVL, unlike Riurik; however, their relationship to one another and to Riurik is unclear. Oleg ruled until 913 when Igor succeeded him, which, if Igor was only one at the time of Riurik's death, would make him thirty-five years old when he is able to succeed.[50] Igor rules until his death in 945, on a raid, at the age of sixty-seven. At Igor's death, his wife Olga (Helga) ruled as regent for their young son Sviatoslav, who came of age and began to rule ca. 964; nineteen years after his father's death. Of course, none of this is impossible, but it does seem unlikely that Oleg ruled as regent, the implication of the chronicle, for thirty plus years, well after his ward's age of majority. That Igor only had one son, and that in his mid-60s, and the son stayed under his mother's rule until he was at least nineteen, if not older. More likely is that the chronicler writing in the eleventh century was attempting to make sense of earlier stories which contained numerous early rulers and to put them into some kind of an order to help ground the ruling clan of Rus.

Oleg has multiple claims to fame, but a key one here is his link between the two bases of Rus. Venturing south from the Rusian base near what will become Novgorod, in 882 he took the city of Kyiv on the Dnieper. Kyiv at the time was ruled by two Scandinavians, Askold and Dir.[51] The PVL ascribes the Rusian attack on Constantinople in the 860s to them, including Photius's dispatch of the Rusians by dipping the hem of a garment of the Mother of God into the Black Sea, causing a storm to rise up and wipe out "the godless Rusians."[52] The PVL's account of this attack is much different than the attacks led by Oleg or Igor in the

[48] R. Zakharii, "The Historiography of Normanist and Anti-Normanist theories on the origin of Rus': A Review of Modern Historiography and Major Sources on Varangian Controversy and Other Scandinavian Concepts of the Origins of Rus'" (University of Oslo: Centre for Viking and Medieval Studies, The Faculty of Arts, 2002).

[49] PVL, s.a. 879. [50] PVL, s.a. 913. [51] PVL, s.a 882.

[52] PVL, s.a. 866. Patriarch Photius also discusses this attack in his homilies. Mango, *The Homilies of Photius,* Homilies 3 and 4 (pp. 82–110).

tenth century, both of whom were also "godless Rusians." The point being made by the chronicler is articulated by Oleg when he confronts Askold and Dir in 882: "'You are not rulers nor even of a ruling family, though I am from a ruling family' and bringing forward Igor 'and this is the son of Riuirk.'"[53] Reading between the lines of the chronicle account we see numerous Scandinavians in eastern Europe, not just one particular family. Oleg's claim to Kyiv is based on force, but the chronicler includes the justification of his being from a ruling family and his possession of Riurik's son, Igor; even though Igor would not come to rule for another thirty-one years. Denigrating Askold and Dir as ignoble also allowed the chronicler to explain the failure of the Rusian attack on Constantinople in the 860s, situating Rus in wider medieval history, but also not denigrating his sponsors who claimed descent from Igor, if not Oleg.

The polity ruled by Oleg stretched from Kyiv in the south to Novgorod in the north and the PVL says that "The Varangians, Slavs, and others who accompanied him were called Rusians."[54] Thus we see already a concatenation of terms wherein Rusian describes not just the Scandinavians but all those under their rule; a key concept in the Normanist controversy. Rus was made up of numerous groups named in the chronicle, all of whom were required to pay tribute to the ruler. Oleg's first task after taking Kyiv was raids on the Derevlians, Severians, and Radimichians to subjugate them.[55] Whether these are really tribal names of the time or were added in later given their formulaic content – the first two names mean forest dwellers and northerners – is unknown. When Igor succeeded to the throne in 913, he had to do the same, re-subjugating those same groups and convincing them to pay tribute to him. Rule was personal and thus ended at the death of the ruler. The new ruler had to create a personal tie of obligation to the subordinate groups. Centralization of political power would not come to Rus until the time of Volodimer Sviatoslavich and was, in many ways, concomitant with the arrival of Christianity.

Oleg and Igor both led raids on Constantinople and both of those raids resulted in treaties interpolated into the PVL. Raids on Constantinople are not surprising given its preeminence in western Eurasia. What might be surprising, however, are the treaties which were created between Rus and the medieval Roman Empire. The treaties read like modern legal documents in which provision is made for equal punishments and responsibility under the law for both "Rusians" and "Christians," which the treaty uses for the Romans.[56] The old Rhodian sea law governing wrecked ships is incorporated into the treaties, and there is clear language about slaves, ransoms, theft, and murder. Igor's treaty, which is overall less advantageous for Rus (presumably because the campaign

[53] PVL, s.a. 882. [54] PVL, s.a. 882. [55] PVL, s.a. 883, 884, 885. [56] PVL, s.a. 912.

was less successful) also contains interesting provisions that designated royal agents from Rus required gold seals to identify themselves while merchants had silver seals.[57] Seals are known from Rus, but the treaty also stipulates that the ruler will include a letter with those seals. The documentary history of Rus is sparse and there are no extant textual sources from this period, nor is there a widespread belief that there was textual evidence from this period.[58] And yet, the treaty indicates that the ruler would send a letter and seals to prove the validity of his designated representatives and merchants. Given that the Rusian god Perun is written into the treaty, it seems unlikely that this is a stock treaty that would not have been, or could not have been, adjusted for this usage.

The PVL begins not as an annal but by situating Rus within universal Christian history. "After the flood, the sons of Noah divided the earth among them."[59] These lines are taken from the chronicle of George Hamartolous but reflect the biblical story of the Flood and the subsequent division of land between Noah's sons. Japheth's territory is expanded to include the eastern European territories familiar to the chronicler; specifically, he says, "In the share of Japheth lies Rus."[60] It was essential for a new polity to find ways to legitimize itself, especially in regard to integrating itself into Christian history. The grounding of the earliest Rusian chronicle in biblical history is an essential part of that, but it also required placement in not just the Old, but the New Testament. Thus, the chronicler quickly moved forward in time to present a story of St. Andrew. St. Andrew is known to have traveled and taught around the Black Sea, but the PVL takes this several steps farther. Andrew came to the Rusian Sea and noticing the Dnieper he decided to travel upriver to reach Rome. Traveling to Rome by going north along the Dnieper is an unlikely route, adding thousands of miles to his trip, but the point was not speed, but connecting the territory which would become Rus to an apostle of Christ. Andrew stopped along the river at a series of hills and proclaimed that "a great city will arise" there, and subsequently Kyiv was built on that location. But this was not enough, as he traveled to the location of Novgorod to experience a Slavic sauna. Afterward on to Rome to have audiences marvel at his tale, and not to take too long out of his known itinerary. The point of St. Andrew's journey is one of legitimization and connection. Rus was late to Christianization and was not part of the Roman Empire, but the story of St. Andrew blessing the hills of Kyiv and visiting the saunas of Novgorod, the two poles of the kingdom in the chronicler's time, endowed Rus with a connection to sanctity.

[57] PVL, s.a. 945.

[58] Simon Franklin, *Writing, Society and Culture in Early Rus', c. 950–1300* (Cambridge: Cambridge University Press, 2002).

[59] PVL [60] PVL

However, the chronicler also had to service local interests as well as wider ones. Thus, following the account of St. Andrew, he immediately launches into a folk version of the founding of Kyiv wherein three brothers, and one sister, found the city. Kii, the eldest brother was the eponymous founder of the city and the other two brothers' names grace hills in the city and the sister was Lebed (swan), a river in southern Kyiv which flows into the Dnieper.[61] The chronicler tells his readers that these siblings were ancestors of many current people in Kyiv, providing a rationale for the inclusion of the tale – glorification of some of the current magnates. Taking foundation stories one step further, the chronicler notes that "some ignorant people believe" that Kii was a ferryman, but that is wrong; instead, he was a powerful ruler who travelled to Constantinople and conquered a wide area. Such a tale seems increasingly far-fetched but may have addressed a persistent rumor at the time about a ferry across the river and Kii's humble origins. Origins which would not be good enough for those connected to the chronicler writer who had to balance Rusian rulers, local magnates, and Christian history in creating a foundation for Rus.

2 Religion

Excavations carried out in the region of medieval Zvenigorod, between the upper reaches of the Western Bug and San Rivers, have unearthed fascinating objects indicative of the wide reach of pilgrims from western Rus.[62] An icon of Sts. George and Demetrius made of pewter and from Thessalonica is representative of the traditional understanding of Rusian Christianity. The warrior saints were especially valued in the medieval Roman Empire and in Rus.[63] In the excavation was also a cross made of wood from the eastern Mediterranean, and numerous seashells (see Figure 2) which have been made into pilgrim's tokens.

The seashell is the object given to those making a pilgrimage to Santiago de Compostela in Galicia. The shrine of St. James was one of the most important pilgrimage spots in Christendom, but typically it is seen as only of importance to those in Latin Europe. These finds from the twelfth to the thirteenth centuries suggest that this was not the case; instead, Santiago de Compostela had a much larger reach among the Christian faith community. Further evidence of these broad connections is found in a series of pilgrim inscriptions found in the church

[61] PVL

[62] V. Hupalo, "Khristianskie relikvii palomnikov iz kniazheskogo zvenigoroda," in *V kamne i v bronze: Sbornik statei v chest' Anny Peskovoi*, ed. A. E. Musin and O. A. Shcheglova (St. Petersburg: RAN, 2017), 117–123.

[63] Monica White, *Military Saints in Byzantium and Rus, 900–1200* (Cambridge: Cambridge University Press, 2013).

Figure 2 Seashell from Zvenihorod (courtesy of V. Hupalo)

of St. Gilles in southern France.[64] The graffiti written in Cyrillic and datable to the thirteenth century include examples such as "God help your servant Semki Ninoslavich."[65] Not only is St. Gilles a Benedictine monastery in France, but it is also on the pilgrimage route to Santiago de Compostela providing a further connection between Rusian religious travelers and the far west of Christian Europe. Such an image is at odds with the traditional picture of Rusian religion which is solely oriented around the labels "Orthodox" and "Byzantine," despite much evidence to the contrary. This section will deal with the conversion of Rus and the many religious ties Rus maintained with the wider Christian world to demonstrate their place in Christian Europe and not just an Orthodox oikumene.

Christianization of Rus

It is possible that there was an initial mission to Christianize Rus in the mid-ninth century, as noted in Section 1, however, the widespread conversion of Rus took place in the later tenth century and began with a dyad akin to that of Helena and Constantine.[66] Olga and her grandson Volodimer are the two who brought Christianity to Rus over the course of approximately thirty years. After the death of Olga's husband Igor, she ruled as regent for their young son Sviatoslav.

64 A. M. Gordin, "Zametki o palomnicheskikh graffiti abbatstva sen-zhil'," in *V kamne i v bronze: Sbornik statei v chest' Anny Peskovoi*, ed. A. E. Musin and O. A. Shcheglova (St. Petersburg: RAN, 2017), 95–103.

65 Gordin, "Zametki o palomnicheskikh graffiti abbatstva sen-zhil'," 95.

66 Francis Butler, *Enlightener of Rus': The Image of Vladimir Sviatoslavich Across the Centuries* (Bloomington: Slavica, 2002), 21, 29, 74.

During that time, it is well attested that she both took a trip to Constantinople and that she converted to Christianity, though whether or not it was in Constantinople is an open question. The PVL records her trip to Constantinople in the year 955.[67] Her purpose, according to the Rusian chronicle, was to attain Christian baptism; which she achieved and the patriarch christened her "Helena [Olena – CR], after the ancient empress, mother of the great Constantine." The emperor, identified as "Constantine, son of Leo" gave her gifts and sent her home as his baptismal daughter. The same chronicle entry records that once she was back in Kyiv, the emperor sent to her and asked for what had been promised to him "presents of slaves, wax, and furs, and soldiers." Olga demurred and suggested that if the emperor were to come to Kyiv, she would give him those things, but not otherwise. As far as the PVL is concerned then, Olga was baptized in Constantinople at the hands of the patriarch and the emperor, but the story is more complicated. Olga's visit to Constantinople is recorded in the contemporary *Book of Ceremonies*. This source was compiled at the order of Constantine VII *Porphyrogenitos* to document the various ceremonies required through examples of actual embassies, receptions, and so forth which occurred during his rule. Olga's visit is discussed in detail, including with whom she met and who accompanied her, but there is not a single reference to baptism.[68] Additionally, Olga is referred to as such throughout, rather than by her baptismal name of Helena. This is an oddity in medieval Roman sources which typically use Christian names for people, even those outside of the empire.[69] Olga's companions on the journey also raise questions about the purpose of the trip. She was accompanied by a priest, Gregory, who received a monetary gift from the emperor; but it is entirely unclear where he is from, apart from the fact that he was part of Olga's entourage. While she brought along numerous relations (both male and female) and agents of other Rusian elites, she also brought over forty merchants (forty-three were present at the first reception and forty-four at the second). The presence of such a large number of merchants, twice that listed in the treaty of 944 between Rus and the empire, has given rise to the supposition that the visit to Constantinople was primarily about trade. Finally, two other Greek sources mention this visit John Skylitzes and John Zonaras. Both Skylitzes and Zonaras report that she was baptized in Constantinople, and both also refer to her as Olga (Elga in the sources).[70] All of which muddies the waters rather than clears them.

---

[67] PVL, s.a. 955.

[68] *Constantine Porphyrogennetos: The Book of Ceremonies*, transl. Ann Moffatt and Maxeme Tall (Leiden: Brill, 2012), Bk. 2, ch. 15, 594–598.

[69] A. V. Nazarenko, *Drevniaia Rus' na mezhdunarodnykh putiakh: Mezhdistsiplinarnye ocherki kul'turnykh, torgovykh, politicheskikh sviazei IX-XII vekov* (Moskva: Iazyki Russkoi Kul'tury, 2001), 274.

[70] John Skylitzes, *A Synopsis of Byzantine History, 811–1057*, transl. John Wortley (Cambridge: Cambridge University Press, 2010) Ch. 11, sec. 6, p. 231; John Zonaras, *Epitome Historiarum* (Lipsiae: B. G. Teubneri, 1871) Bk. 16, cap. 22, pp. 68-69.

It is essential then to look elsewhere for information. The Latin sources also contain information about Olga and her baptism, as well as the Christianization of Rus. That they do is a subtle, but important, statement regarding the place of Rus in Christian Europe. The continuator of Regino of Prum notes in the year 959 that an envoy of "Queen Helena of the Rusians," who had been baptized in Constantinople, arrived and asked the Ottonian emperor for a bishop and priests to convert her people.[71] Though brief, this entry adds a great deal to our discussion. Here Olga is referred to by her baptismal name of Helena, the only other source to do so thus far, and her place of baptism is noted as Constantinople, agreeing with the PVL, Skylitzes, and Zonaras. The purpose of the embassy though is of particular note, as she is seeking assistance in conversion from the German Empire. Even basing our understanding solely on Regino's continuator, it is clear that there was an interesting byplay underway in which the Rusian queen sought baptism from one empire and a bishop from another.[72] Otto had a bishop ordained for the mission to Rus the next year, but as he died, it was not until 961 that Bishop Adalbert undertook the mission.[73] "Exhausted" from his toils, Adalbert returned home in 962 unable to report any success in the conversion.[74] Adalbert's lack of success can likely be explained by Sviatoslav's coming of age in Rus. The PVL has him acting on his own as an adult in 964, and it is possible that he was already exercising power before that.[75] Sviatoslav was himself a confirmed pagan who adopted the habits of steppe dress and accoutrement, and told his mother flatly that he would not convert to Christianity as his "followers will laugh at it."[76] Thus, though Olga converted and took the Christian name Helena, Rus as a whole did not convert at this time.

The conversion of Rus to Christianity came about under Olga's grandson, Volodimer Sviatoslavich, though the process was not without exploration of alternate paths. Volodimer first attempted to create his own pantheon of gods out of the existing deities worshipped by the various peoples within Rus.[77] But only a few years later, a set of three entries begin in the PVL detailing three different

---

[71] *Reginonis Abbatis Prumiensis Chronicon cum continuation Treverensi*, ed. Frederick Kurze, in MGH SS 50 (Hannover: Impensis Biblipolii Hahniani, 1890), s.a. 959.

[72] This issue is examined in more detail in a variety of places, including Christian Raffensperger, *Reimagining Europe: Kievan Rus' in the Medieval World* (Cambridge, MA: Harvard University Press, 2012), 156–158.

[73] *Reginonis Abbatis Prumiensis Chronicon cum continuation Treverensi*, s.a. 960, 961.

[74] *Reginonis Abbatis Prumiensis Chronicon cum continuation Treverensi*, s.a. 962.

[75] PVL, s.a. 964. This is the next entry after that of 955 which details Olga's baptism. The nearly decade-long gap may mean something in this regard, or, of course, it may not.

[76] PVL, s.a. 955.

[77] PVL, s.a. 980. For more on these gods, see Simon Franklin and Jonathan Shepard, *The Emergence of Rus, 750–1200* (New York: Longman, 1996), 155.

conversion stories, which it seems the chronicler, writing in the late eleventh or early twelfth century, was attempting to put together into a whole. The stories articulate a search for a monotheistic faith from amongst Judaism, Islam, and Christianity, exploring both German and Constantinopolitan variants. Judaism is dismissed largely out of hand after the first story in 986, and the others are investigated more thoroughly.[78] Though Volodimer does not convert to Islam, there is a substantial presence of Rus in Islamic sources discussing this possibility, something not taken as seriously by the Christian authors of the PVL.[79] For those authors, the choice comes down to which variant of Christianity? The PVL lauds Constantinopolitan Christianity, spending pages on enlightening Volodimer, and the reader, on the intricacies of faith and the history of church councils, while also describing the interior of Hagia Sophia as heavenly compared to the lack of "glory" found in the German churches.[80] Despite these pages devoted to the faith, what converts Volodimer is, as might be expected, a miracle, though one connected with dynastic marriage. Under the year 988, Volodimer captured the Roman city of Cherson with the aid of a mole inside the city named Anastasius.[81] He then offered to give the city back to emperors Basil II and Constantine VIII in exchange for the hand of their sister Anna *Porphyrogenita* in marriage. The emperors agreed, but stipulated that Volodimer must first be baptized. Anna was delivered to Volodimer in Cherson where, failing to immediately convert, he was struck blind.[82] Volodimer converted at Anna's behest, and he was subsequently healed. According to the PVL, the couple returned to Kyiv and Volodimer baptized his population in the Dnieper River Christianizing Rus.

The story beyond the PVL's telling is, as one might imagine, slightly more complicated. Procopius records that a band of Rusians (Tauroscythians) came to Constantinople in 988 to aid Basil II in putting down uprisings against his rule.[83] That these troops were sent by Volodimer is confirmed by the Egyptian Melkite Christian, Yaḥya Ibn Sa'īd (d. c.1066) who recorded that Basil II faced a revolt of one of his nobles and asked for assistance from the Rusian king, to whom he gave his sister in marriage.[84] Ibn Sa'īd also notes the baptism of

[78] PVL, s.a. 986.

[79] Andriy Danylenko explores this more in "Rus' and the South" with Christian Raffensperger, *Encyclopedia of Slavic Languages and Linguistics*, ed. Marc L. Greenberg (Leiden: Brill, 2024 [forthcoming])

[80] PVL, s.a. 987. [81] PVL, s.a. 988.

[82] For an excellent analysis of these stories and the blinding see Donald Ostrowski, "The Account of Volodimer's Conversion in the *Povest' vremennykh let*: A Chiasmus of Stories," *Harvard Ukrainian Studies* 28:1–4 (2006 [actually 2010]), 567–580.

[83] Michael Psellos, *Fourteen Byzantine Rulers: The Chronographia of Michael Psellus*, transl. E. R. A. Sewter (New York: Penguin, 1966), bk 1 14–15.

[84] *Histoire de Yahya-ibn-Sa'īd d'Antioche*, transl. I. Kratchkovsky et A. Vasiliev part 2, 423.

Volodimer and his kingdom, as well, and the building of many churches there. Using these sources, it is possible to expand the story offered to this: Basil II needed troops to assist in putting down the revolt of Bardas Phocas. In exchange for troops, Volodimer asked for Anna *Porphyrogenita's* hand in marriage, and despite the fact that she was desired as a prospective bride by both the Ottonian and Capetian royal families, Basil II had no choice but to marry her to the pagan Volodimer. Volodimer sent troops to assist Basil II, but Anna was not forthcoming and thus Volodimer besieged and took the city of Cherson, holding it for ransom until Anna arrived there, at which time the city was returned to Constantinopolitan control (as a "wedding present" according to the PVL).[85] The pieces fit well in this order and it helps us understand the political rationale for both Volodimer's and Rusian conversion in order to placate the Roman emperors and Volodimer's new wife.

The PVL records that "the bishop of Cherson and the priests of the princess (Anna)" were the ones who baptized Volodimer; perhaps tellingly, nothing about the baptism is recorded in Roman sources.[86] Following his baptism and marriage, he gathered "Anastasius and the priests of Cherson" along with the relics of St. Clement and several bronze statutes and returned to Kyiv. There is no mention in the PVL, nor in Greek sources, of a missionary bishop being sent from Constantinople, though Ibn Sa'īd does mention that a metropolitan was sent.[87] The provenance of the relics of St. Clement are an interesting, and still open, question. Constantine / Cyril, on his journey in the Black Sea to attempt the conversion of the Khazars, came upon the relics of St. Clement in the mid-ninth century. He carried those relics with him on his journey and eventually all the way to Rome.[88] That the relics appeared again in Cherson is odd, unless one gives credence to a later Rusian source which indicates that an embassy was sent to Volodimer from the papacy while he was in Cherson and it bore holy relics.[89] The relics of St. Clement could play on Volodimer from multiple angles: as a tie to the papacy given Clement's position as third successor to St. Peter; a connection to the Black Sea where Clement was exiled and the relics were found; a tie to the Apostle to the Slavs himself St. Cyril; and finally, relics of his new religion which had the power to create miracles. Whatever their origin, they became prominent relics in Rus and, according to Thietmar of Merseburg, Volodimer erected a church in Kyiv for them and this was where he and Anna were buried.[90] This church is not recorded in the PVL which suggests that the

[85] PVL, s.a. 988. [86] PVL, s.a. 988.

[87] *Histoire de Yahya-ibn-Sa'īd d'Antioche*, transl. I. Kratchkovsky et A. Vasiliev part 2, 423.

[88] Francis Dvornik, *Byzantine Missions among the Slavs* (New Brunswick: Rutgers University Press, 1970), 66, 137–138.

[89] Nikon Chronicle, p. 57.

[90] *Ottonian Germany: The "Chronicon" of Thietmar of Merseburg*, transl. David A. Warner (Manchester: Manchester University Press, 2001), Bk. 7, ch. 74.

first church he built in the city was dedicated to his patron St. Basil and the next year he built the Tithe Church in Kyiv which he entrusted to Anastasius of Cherson.[91] Volodimer also "appointed priests from Cherson" to the church and gave it the appropriated goods from that city, perhaps including the relics of St. Clement. Anastasius is known only as the betrayer of Cherson in the PVL, and yet he is here appointed to one of the first churches in Rus with a staff of priests from Cherson. There is no evidence in the PVL that there was a Constantinopolitan metropolitan directing affairs, rather Volodimer himself was the agent behind such appointments; and later the royal family itself was responsible for founding churches and appointing priests, as was common throughout medieval Europe.

The first mention of a metropolitan in Rus is when Metropolitan Theopemptos consecrated a new church in 1039.[92] There is no recorded metropolitan before this time, though much debate exists on this topic. The record of metropolitans is incomplete with multiple gaps of years with no mention of anyone serving in that office, especially in the eleventh century. The majority of metropolitans were appointed to Kyiv by the patriarch of Constantinople. It is widely assumed that they were unable to speak the local language and, in fact, little is known of any of their life and career before their appointments until the middle of the twelfth century.[93] In the mid-eleventh century, late in his tenure as ruler, Iaroslav Volodimerich created the first native Rusian metropolitan, Ilarion.[94] The language of the PVL is quite interesting as it says that "Iaroslav, after assembling the bishops, appointed Ilarion as metropolitan in Holy Sophia [the metropolitan church in Kyiv]." This is the entirety of the information provided in the chronicle about his appointment and thus it seems that it was Iaroslav himself who did the appointing and thus the episode has been connected with the 1043 Rusian attack on Constantinople and a disjunction in relations.[95] Ilarion does not seem to have been metropolitan long, but he is well-known for his "Sermon on Law and Grace" which integrates Rus into biblical history.[96] After Iaroslav's death, Rus enters

---

91 PVL, s.a. 988, 989. 92 PVL, s.a. 1039.

93 Andrzej Poppe, "Leontios, Abbot of Patmos, Candidate for the Metropolitan See of Rus'," in *Christian Russia in the Making* (Aldershot: Ashgate Variorum, 2007), 1–13. "Metropolitan Nicephorus, early in the twelfth century, expressed regret that he had to 'stand speechless among you' for lack of knowledge of the language." Jonathan Shepard, "Rus'" in *Christianization and the Rise of Christian Monarchy: Scandinavia, Central Europe and Rus', c. 900–1200*, ed. Nora Berend (Cambridge: Cambridge University Press, 2007): 401.

94 PVL, s.a. 1051.

95 Wider context on this event is provided in Jonathan Shepard, "Why Did the Russians Attack Byzantium in 1043?" *Byzantinisch-Neugriechische Jahrbücher* 22, ed. Nikos A. Bees (Athens: Verlag de BNJ, 1985), 147–212.

96 Ilarion, "Sermon on Law and Grace," in *Sermons and Rhetoric of Kievan Rus'*, transl. Simon Franklin (Cambridge, MA: Harvard University Press, 1991), 3–30.

a period in which it has three metropolitans for a period of time, and it is unknown which of them, if any, were appointed from Constantinople. In 1055, the Novgorod First Chronicle records the presence of a Metropolitan Ephraim.[97] An Ephraim appears later as a Rusian monk, and eunuch, who traveled to Constantinople to experience monastic life there, and was the source of the Stoudite Rule in Rus.[98] He then became metropolitan of Pereiaslavl while there were also metropolitans for both Kyiv and Chernigov in the 1070s and 1080s. Attempting to make sense of this troika of metropolitans has bedeviled historians for generations, resulting in numerous theories.[99] The See of Rhosia was the single largest metropolitanate subordinate to the patriarch of Constantinople, and yet the patriarchs were unwilling to divide it, as is seen several times in the twelfth to fourteenth centuries.[100] The PVL records a Metropolitan Georgios in 1073 only by noting that he was absent in the Roman Empire at that time, and then the next mention of a metropolitan is Ioann in 1086.[101] The entry for 1089 encapsulates part of the problem with who was metropolitan and when as it notes that Metropolitan Ioann died; that Ianka Vsevolodovna was sent to Constantinople for a new metropolitan (also named Ioann), and that "Ephraim, the metropolitan of that church" consecrated "the Church of St. Michael in Pereiaslavl."[102] The entry continues with a listing of the ecclesiastical deeds of Ephraim in that region. But then, in 1091, Ephraim is listed under a series of "bishops" and in the *Paterik of the Kyivan Caves Monastery* he is only listed as a bishop.[103] Affairs become slightly more regular and better documented in the twelfth century, for instance we know a good deal about the career of Metropolitan Constantine II in the 1160s as he disciplined the monks of the Caves Monastery and mutilated Bishop Feodor of Suzdal.[104]

The role of the metropolitan of Kyiv as the leader of the Church and delegate of the patriarch of Constantinople leaves more questions than answers when the

[97] There is no metropolitan present at Iaroslav's death just a few years later (1054), and in 1055 the Novgorod First Chronicle records the presence of a Metropolitan Ephrem. PVL, s.a. 1054, NPL, s.a. 1055.

[98] *The Paterik of the Kievan Caves Monastery*, transl. Muriel Heppell (Cambridge, MA: Harvard Ukrainian Research Institute, 1989), Discours 8 (pp. 41, 44). For more on Ephraim see D. G. Khrustalev, *Razyskaniia o Efreme Pereiaslavskom* (Sankt-Peterburg: Evraziia, 2002).

[99] For two examples, with representative citations, see A. V. Poppe, "Russkie mitropolii konstantinopol'skoi patriarkhii v XI stoletii," *Vizantiiskii Vremennik* 28 (1968): 98–104; A.V. Nazarenko, "Mitropolii iaroslavichei vo vtoroi polovine XI veka," in *Drevniaia Rus' i Slaviane* (Moscow: RAN, 2009), 207–245.

[100] Christian Raffensperger and Donald Ostrowski, *The Ruling Families of Rus: Clan, Family, and Kingdom* (London: Reaktion Books, 2023), 213–216.

[101] PVL, s.a. 1073, 1086. [102] PVL, s.a. 1089.

[103] PVL, s.a. 1091; *The Paterik of the Kievan Caves Monastery*, Discourse 9 (p. 92).

[104] Poppe, "Leontios, Abbot of Patmos," 9–10. He was so harsh, in fact, that he was recalled to Constantinople and replaced in 1170.

source base is examined. It is widely accepted by scholars that the PVL was written by monks who were part of a Church hierarchy which reported to a metropolitan of Kyiv.[105] Despite that belief, the chronicle record is surprisingly uninterested in the affairs of the metropolitans. Combined with the lack of updates to the menologia with the names of patriarchs post-ninth century, it is possible to suggest that the ecclesiastical relationship between Rus and Constantinople was not nearly as strong in the eleventh to twelfth centuries as is widely imagined.[106]

Gertrude's Psalter

One of the most well-known women of medieval Rus is Gertrude, the Polish princess who became the wife of Iziaslav Iaroslavich in the middle of the eleventh century. Gertrude appears in almost no textual sources by name, and yet she left behind a marvelous testament to her existence and her faith. The Gertrude Psalter, also referred to as the Egbert or Trier Psalter, began life in the Ottonian Empire in the tenth century and came into Gertrude's possession via her mother, Richeza, a member of the Ottonian family.[107] In Rus, Gertrude added a number of prayers to the codex as well as several images.[108] For all of these, she was the maker, to use Therese Martin's evocative term which points out the "false dichotomy" in modern scholarship between artist and patron (which itself is gendered male); instead noting that medieval inscriptions used "made" (*fecit*) for those who physically constructed something as well as for those who paid for said construction.[109] Gertrude's Psalter, the pieces composed in Rus and made by her, then are statements of her faith.

---

[105] For instance, Omeljan Pritsak suggests that there is evidence of Metropolitan Nikephoras's influence in the compilation of the PVL in the early twelfth century. *The Old Rus' Kievan and Galician-Volhynian Chronicles: The Ostroz'kyj (Xlebnikov) and četvertyns'kyj (Pogodin) codices*, Omeljan Pritsak, Introduction (Cambridge, MA: Harvard University Press, 1990), xvi.

[106] While specialists may question the accuracy of this claim regarding "widely imagined," I would point to one of the best textbooks on medieval Europe which states that "Choosing Christianity linked Russia to the West, but choosing the Byzantine form guaranteed that Russia would always stand apart from Western Europe." Barbara H. Rosenwein, *A Short History of the Middle Ages* (Toronto: University of Toronto Press, 2009 [3rd ed.]), 147.

[107] Natalia Anna Makaryk Zajac, "Women between West and East: The Inter-Rite Marriages of the Kyivan Rus' Dynasty, ca. 1000–1204" (PhD Dissertation; University of Toronto, 2017), 108, 126, 135.

[108] Gertrude "commissioned ninety-five additional Latin prayers to be added to Egbert's Psalter for her personal use, as well as five miniatures" most likely in the period after the death of Iziaslav (d. 1078) and the before the death of her son Iaropolk (d. 1086/87)." Zajac, "Women between West and East," 108.

[109] Therese Martin, "Exceptions and Assumptions: Women in Medieval Art History," in *Reassessing the Roles of Women as "Makers" of Medieval Art and Architecture*, ed. Therese Martin (Leiden: Brill, 2012), 2.

Gertrude was a devout Christian with a particular devotion to St. Peter, which may have been because of her son Iaropolk's visit to the papacy in the early 1070s, or because that was his Christian name.[110] One of the images in the Psalter is of St. Peter (Figure 3).

Gertrude herself appears in this image, one of only a few examples of an image of a medieval Rusian woman we can identify. She is not named, however. The label above her head reads simply "Mother of Iaropolk." "Mother" is a ligature and could be Greek, but "Iaropolk" is written clearly in Slavonic. Gertrude herself is performing proskynesis, the traditional donor, ktetor, pose at the base of St. Peter, clasping his foot. Given all that we understand about medieval art composition, she is identified here as the maker of this work. The work itself is exceptional and simply examining this one page will highlight Gertrude's religious experience which crosses what moderns have divided into separate faith traditions.

Gertrude came from the "Latin" world as a Polish princess and the psalter itself has its origins in the German Empire. It is no surprise then that the text of the psalter, even the 95 prayers added in Rus, are in Latin. The prayers on this page are clearly made with the shape of the illumination in mind as they conform to the space provided on St. Peter's right and left. The prayer to his left (the right of the page) has been seen as Gertrude's direct address to St. Peter:

> O Saint Peter, prince of the Apostles, who holds the keys of the kingdom of heaven; through that love by which You loved and love the Lord, and through His sweetest mercy by which God mercifully looked down on you as you wept bitterly over your triple denial, mercifully look upon me the unworthy handmaiden of Christ; absolve the bonds of all my vices and crimes.[111]

Gertrude herself is the "unworthy handmaiden of Christ" and thus along with her image as donor, she appears twice on this page of the psalter. Talia Zajac has pointed out the Latin elements in this prayer such as the "keys of the kingdom of heaven." While there were some instances of the presence of keys related to St. Peter in medieval Roman iconography, it was largely confined to the western tradition as a way to recognize St. Peter as the first pope. In the image of St. Peter on the page one can also see the keys in his left hand, along with a scroll, reinforcing the textual description of the keys.

A connection with the papacy may also be made here via the presence of Iaropolk and his wife Cunigunda, the two figures at St. Peter's left receiving

[110] Members of the ruling clan in Rus had both Christian and Slavic names, as well as sometimes nicknames. We typically refer to them by their Slavic names, but know many of their Christian or baptismal names from the chronicle record.

[111] Zajac, "Women between West and East," 138. The translation is from Zajac who is also preparing a full translation of the psalter.

Figure 3 St. Peter Gertrude Codex – Cividale del Friuli, Museo Archeologico Nazionale, Archivi e Biblioteca, codex CXXXVI)

his blessing. In 1073, Iziaslav was expelled as the ruler of Rus and taking Gertrude and their son Iaropolk, fled first to Poland and then to the German Empire. While Iziaslav appealed for help to Henry IV at Mainz, Iaropolk, and his new German bride Cunigunda, were sent to Rome to meet with Pope

Gregory VII. The pope listened to Iaropolk's plea and granted the kingdom of Rus to Iziaslav, via Iaropolk, in exchange for fidelity to the papacy.[112] Pope Gregory VII then sent a papal legate with the Rusian family to deliver a message, and possibly a crown, to Bolesław II of Poland who subsequently assisted Iziaslav to return home and regain rule in Rus.[113] At Iaropolk's death in 1086, the Rusian chronicler records that he had built a church dedicated to St. Peter, the first of its kind in Rus.[114] Numerous scholars have discussed the possibility of a conversion of Iaropolk to Latin Christianity or possible dedication to the papacy, but it is important to clarify that conversion was not required at this time and in fact what is seen here is evidence of the "big tent" of Christian Europe.[115]

Gertrude's psalter as a whole provides additional evidence of this "big tent" or perhaps simply the lack of the hard dividing lines which we imagine existed in the medieval past. The image of St. Peter in Figure 3 is largely medieval Roman in composition. A contemporary medallion made in Constantinople shows the same bust image of St. Peter with eyes shifting to the viewer's right.[116] The medallion is clearly labeled "o agios Petros" on either side of the saint's head, something which is present, but difficult to see in the psalter page. The Latin prayers of Gertrude are original (to the saint's left) and a borrowing from an Anglo-Saxon prayer (to the saint's right).[117] And thus, the image is representative of Gertrude's life and wider faith tradition in Rus: Latin, Greek, and Slavonic text on one page. Medieval Roman design elements mixed with those from the Latin West. All combined into one whole.

Though Gertrude has been given, and deserves, immense credit for the psalter; the Christian life of Rus was not strictly oriented toward the Roman Empire or away from the West, in general. One place where this is abundantly clear is in the celebration of saints' days in Rus. Over time, certain saints worshipped throughout the Christian world began to be celebrated on different days in different places. In Rus, we see a mix of medieval Roman and Latin days

[112] H. E. J. Cowdrey, *Pope Gregory VII 1073–1085* (Oxford: Clarendon Press, 1998), 452–453.

[113] *The Register of Pope Gregory VII, 1073–1085*, Ed. and transl. H. E. J. Cowdrey (Oxford: Oxford University Press, 2002), 2.73 – for Gregory's subtle letter to Bolesław chiding him for stealing his in-law Iziaslav's money and expelling him.

[114] PVL, s.a. 1086.

[115] There is a great deal of analysis of Iaropolk and Gertrude. For a sampling see V. L. Ianin, "Russkaia kniaginia Olisava-Gertruda i ee syn Iaropolk," *Numizmatika i epigrafika* 4 (1963): 142–164; N. I. Shchaveleva, "Kniaz' Iaropolk Iziaslavich i khristianskaia tserkov' XI v," in *Vostochnaia evropa v drevnosti I srednevekov'e: X Cheteniia k 80-letiiu chlena-korrespondenta AN SSSR Vladimira Terent'evicha Pashuto*. E. A. Mel'nikova, ot. Red. (Moscow: RAN, 1998): 132–136; Nazarenko, *Drevniaia Rus' na mezhdunarodnykh putiakh*, 559–584.

[116] www.metmuseum.org/art/collection/search/464543.

[117] The prayer is largely Alcuin of York's "For the Gift of Tears."

in the menologia. The earliest Rusian menologion is the Ostromir Gospel, created for the eponymous mayor of Novgorod in 1056/1057.[118] It contains several saints' days which accord with the Latin calendar rather than that of Constantinople, including Silvester, Polikarp, and Vitus.[119] The second oldest menologion is contained in the Archangel Gospel of 1092.[120] This, too, contains divergent dates for saints, but different saints than had appeared with Western dates in the Ostromir Gospel. The Archangel Gospel lists Latin dates for the Apostle Paul, the martyrs Kosmas and Damian and several others.[121] In addition, it contains a listing for St. Wenceslaus who does not appear in Constantinopolitan menologia.[122] Dated to the third quarter of the eleventh century is a birchbark document from Novgorod which contains a list of saints and saints' days, though all are in keeping with the Constantinopolitan calendar.[123] Finally, coming back to the Gertrude Psalter, it contains the same feast days as the Ostromir Gospel, perhaps suggesting a common origin.[124] One thing that the Rusian menologia have in common is that they do not contain sainted patriarchs after Nikifor who died in 828.[125] A glaring omission given the modern understanding of the relationship between the churches.

Rusian religious books also give us another glimpse into an appropriation of Western design, the symbols of the evangelists. Drawing on the Book of Revelation, early Church Fathers created symbols for each of the gospel writers. The most commonly used set in medieval Europe was that created by St. Jerome comprising: the Lion for Saint Mark, Angel for Saint Matthew, the Eagle for Saint John, and the Ox for Saint Luke. Typically, medieval Roman illuminated manuscripts do not include the symbols for the evangelists.[126] When symbols

[118] A scanned image of the manuscript is available only at: http://nlr.ru/eng/exib/Gospel/ostr/index.html.

[119] O. V. Loseva, *Russkie Mesiateslovy XI–XIV vekov* (Moscow: Pamiatniki istoricheskoi mysli, 2001), 64–65.

[120] For a brief introduction to the source in English see: https://blog.lib.utah.edu/book-of-the-week-arkhangel-skoe-evanglie-1092-goda/.

[121] Loseva, *Russkie Mesiateslovy*, 66.

[122] Francis Butler, "Wenceslas: The Saint and His Name in Kievan Rus," *Slavic and East European Journal* 48:1 (2004): 64–66.

[123] http://gramoty.ru/birchbark/document/show/novgorod/913/. For analysis and explication see Ildar H. Garipzanov, "Novgorod and the Veneration of Saints in Eleventh-Century Rus': A Comparative View," in *Saints and Their Lives on the Periphery: Veneration of Saints in Scandinavia and Eastern Europe (c. 1000–1200)*, ed. Haki Antonsson and Ildar H. Garipzanov (Turnhout, Belgium: Brepols, 2010), 121.

[124] Loseva, *Russkie Mesiateslovy*, 65; Olenka Z. Pevny, "Kievan Rus'," in *The Glory of Byzantium: Art and Culture of the Middle Byzantine Era, A.D. 843–1261*, ed. Helen C. Evans and William D. Wixom (New York: Metropolitan Museum of Art, 1997): 296.

[125] Loseva, *Russkie Mesiateslovy*, 60.

[126] Robert S. Nelson, *The Iconography of Preface and Miniature in the Byzantine Gospel Book* (New York: New York University Press for the College Art Association, 1980), 15.

for the evangelists do appear, they do not often follow the Hieronymic model. Instead, there are other pairings of evangelist and symbol, such as that of Epiphanios: Matthew – Man; Mark – Calf; Luke – Lion; John – Eagle.[127] This format can also be seen in the Georgian Gelati Gospels which were composed on Mt. Athos during the late Komnenian period.[128] Rusian manuscripts of the eleventh to twelfth centuries, however, both depict the evangelists with symbols and they regularly, and only, use the Hieronymic system. The Ostromir Gospel has images of the three of the evangelists preserved, Mark, John, and Luke.[129] The image of Luke can be seen in Figure 4.

The portrayal of Luke has many similarities to that of St. Peter in the Gertrude Psalter; in terms of the chrysographia and bright colors evocative of the cloisonne enamel which was so prized by the Rusians. What stands out, however, is the ox appearing in the upper right-hand corner, handing the parchment to St. Luke; the ox being the Hieronymic symbol for St. Luke. The same can be seen in the illumination of St. Luke from the twelfth-century Mstislav Lectionary (Figure 5).[130]

Though the artistic style has altered slightly, all of the stylistic elements have been retained, inclusive of the ox handing St. Luke the unrolled scroll. Returning full circle to the Gertrude Psalter, we can see the symbols of the evangelists there as well (Figure 6).

In the image of Christ Enthroned (Figure 6), he has above him all four of the symbols of the evangelists; perhaps with a stylistic pairing of the tetramorphs below him as well. The Gertrude Psalter is well known as an object which is representative of a Latin woman bearing her religious identity in Rus. But the Ostromir Gospel and the other texts examined in this section have no such personal connection to a Latin figure, male or female; and yet, they too bear the hallmarks of coming from an ecumenical Christian environment not dependent upon Constantinople. What we might then suggest is that the Rusian Christian world was a syncretic one where Christian elements came from the medieval Roman Empire, but also from Poland, Hungary, the German Empire, Anglo-Saxon England and elsewhere along with the many visitors, traders, and spouses to Rus.

In the early twelfth century, a Rusian monk named Daniil traveled to Jerusalem on pilgrimage. He left a record of his journey which describes

---

[127] Nelson, *The Iconography of Preface and Miniature*, 18.

[128] Nelson, *The Iconography of Preface and Miniature*, 20. See also Sh. J. Amiranashvili, *Georgian Art* (Tbilisi: Tbilisi University Press, 1968), 19–20.

[129] There is a deeper discussion of these images in O. S. Popova, "Ostromirovo evangelie. Miniatiury i ornamenty," in *Ostromirovo evangelie i sovremennye issledovaniia. Rukopisnoi traditsii. Novozavetnykh tekstov*, ed. S. A. Daydova (Saint Petersburg: Rossiiskaia natsional'-naia biblioteka, 2010), 6084.

[130] Available online via the Russian State Historical Museum – shm.ru.

Figure 4 Miniature of St. Luke from the Ostromir Lectionary (Russian National Library)

distances traveled, churches and wonders seen, as well as his reception in the city itself. At this time, Jerusalem had been taken by the First Crusade, which received no mention in the Rusian chronicle record.[131] Baldwin was king and given the timing of the pilgrimage in 1107-1108 it is likely that this was during the interregnum before Ghibellin of Arles became patriarch in 1108. Baldwin welcomed Daniil to Jerusalem and took him to pray at the Church of the Holy Sepulchre.[132] Daniil refers to Baldwin as "my ruler [*kniaz'*] and my lord" when thanking him for his graciousness. Daniil then processes into the church with

[131] Nazarenko discusses this briefly and notes where there are two allusions to the conquest of Jerusalem. *Drevniaia Rus' na mezhdunarodnykh putiakh*, 627.

[132] "Khozhenie Daniila, igumena Russkoi zemli." in *Kniga khozhenii: Zapiski russkikh puteshestvennikov XI–XV vv.* (Moscow: Sovetskaia Rossiia, 1984), 73–74.

Figure 5 Miniature of St. Luke from the Mstislav Lectionary (Russian National Library)

Baldwin and the abbot of St. Sabas monastery where he watches the service. Daniil designates the priests at the high altar as "Latin" and notes that they began "to squeal" their prayers, as opposed to those of the correct faith ("*pravovernii*") who sang Vespers. This is the only derogatory mention of the Latins in Daniil's text, and one can surmise that it has as much to do with the sound of the Latin chant as anything else. Unfamiliar sounds have often been described in such ways, witness the Greek label for barbarians – those who make a ba-ba sound, or the Slavs label for Germans – *nemtsy* – those who cannot speak. Daniil records that Baldwin, whom he addresses with the same title (*kniaz'*) as he does Rusian rulers, allows him to record the names of the rulers who sent him and points out that all that happened can be affirmed by the other Rusians on the journey, several of whom he names. Daniil's visit is indicative of

Figure 6 Miniature of Christ enthroned, folio 10v (Gertrude Codex – Cividale del Friuli, Museo Archeologico Nazionale, Archivi e Biblioteca, codex CXXXVI)

the broad Christian ecumenism present in Rusian belief that differs from the invective recorded in some texts, including the PVL during Volodimer's conversion.[133] There is little idea in Daniil's text of tension between the various Christianities nor hostility about a Latin patriarch.

133 PVL, s.a. 988. For instance, where it says, "Do not accept the teachings of the Latins, whose instruct is vicious."

The crusades in the eastern Mediterranean were of little interest, at least according to preserved writings, to the Rusians. The sack of Constantinople in 1204 by the Fourth Crusade is recorded in some detail by the Novgorod Chronicle, though the account is focused upon, and bookended by, the struggle between Roman contenders for the throne.[134] There is no religious animus against Latins or for Orthodox. The sacking of churches is mentioned and condemned, simply because they are churches. For the lived experience of the people of Rus, the separation from the Latin world really occurs with the activities of the papal legate, William of Sabina. In 1222, Pope Honorius III declared that Orthodox churches should be closed in all Latin lands. This was not a problem in most places, as there were few in the majority of Western Europe. However, in the Baltic, both Christianities had coexisted for some time, as is seen by the presence of Latin churches to St. Olaf in Novgorod, and Rusian churches on Gotland.[135] The impact of Pope Honorius' edict came with the Latin conquest of Dorpat in 1224. Dorpat had strong ties with Novgorod and there were Orthodox churches within its borders, all of which were closed. William of Sabina also ordered proselytization of the Orthodox population. The combination of these factors led to a disruption in the Novgorodian lands and Iaroslav Vsevolodich, ruler of Novgorod, attacked Dorpat in 1234.[136] Legate William responded by agitating the papacy for a crusade directed against Rus, which Pope Gregory IX granted in 1240. A clear rift between Latin and Orthodox had been created, and yet even after that time, there were still some who managed to exist between those worlds, trading and working for both parties.[137]

3 The Kingdom of Rus: From the Inside

The idea of Rus as a kingdom, as an organized polity even, is rare in the secondary scholarship. An essential element in a series focused on "Rethinking" polities is attempting to understand and articulate how Rus functioned as a kingdom and how it was governed. This section divides the issue into two; first dealing with the existence of a "kingdom" of Rus, and the title of the Rusian ruler; second is a brief

[134] *Novgorod Chronicle,* s.a. 1204.

[135] Tatjana N. Jackson, "The Cult of St Olaf and Early Novgorod," in *Saints and Their Lives on the Periphery: Veneration of Saints in Scandinavia and Eastern Europe (c. 1000–1200)*, ed. Haki Antonsson and Ildar H. Garipzanov (Turnhout, Belgium: Brepols, 2010), 147–170; Anthony Cutler, "Garda, Källunge and the Byzantine Tradition on Gotland," *Art Bulletin* 51:3 (1969): 257–266.

[136] Novgorod Chronicle, s.a. 1234.

[137] Anti Selart does a terrific job of problematizing the hard and fast lines of Orthodox and Latin in the lived experience of people in the Baltic in *Livonia, Rus' and the Baltic Crusades in the Thirteenth Century*, transl. Fiona Robb (Leiden and Boston: Brill, 2015).

look at what governance looked like in Rus via the various positions which made up the court and the functionaries in the kingdom.

Titles – From Prince to King

In the early thirteenth century, Henry of Livonia wrote about the ongoing conflict in the Baltic between the local Livs, the Rusians on the other side of Lake Chud (Peipus), and the newly arrived Germans and their crusaders. Rus is interwoven into Henry's narrative as the various Rusian rulers played a major role in Baltic affairs. Henry says, "the great king of Novgorod, and likewise the king of Polotsk, came with their Russians in a great army . . . "[138] "King Vladimir went with these Letts . . . "[139] and later "the Russians kings . . . "[140] Throughout his chronicle, Henry refers to the rulers of Rus as kings, using "*rex*" or "*reges*."[141] James Brundage who has translated the chronicle into English, uses "king" in his translation, but then adds a footnoted caveat early in the text: "Vladimir was a Russian prince, not a king, as Henry calls him."[142] And slightly later "Like the 'king' of Polozk, the 'king' of Gerzika was a Russian prince."[143] Brundage was a historian of medieval canon law and entered crusade studies from that angle. To help him with unfamiliar territories and peoples, like all good scholars, he turned to existing scholarship and definitions. Though Brundage first published his translation in 1961, the Columbia UP edition is from 2003 and he could have used Simon Franklin and Jonathan Shepard's *The Emergence of Rus* for the revised notes, as they use "prince" as the title for the Rusian rulers throughout. So does Janet Martin's *Medieval Russia*, at least when speaking of the Kyivan period.[144] Even if Brundage would have turned to an expert on Russian history, for that is the designation both in the book and which is largely common still in the field, he would have found that a simple translation of the word "*kniaz*'" into English is "prince."[145] However, I would suggest, and have,[146] that the medieval Rusian ruler's title should be translated

[138] Henricus Lettus, *The Chronicle of Henry of Livonia*, transl. James A. Brundage (New York: Columbia University Press, 2003), bk. 4, ch. XIV.

[139] Henricus Lettus, *The Chronicle of Henry of Livonia*, Bk. 4, ch. XVI.

[140] Henricus Lettus, *The Chronicle of Henry of Livonia*, Bk. 4, ch. XXVII.

[141] Henricus Lettus, *Heinrici Chronicion Lyvoniae*, ed. Wilhelm Arndt (Hannover: Impensis Bibliopolii Hahniani, 1874).

[142] Henricus Lettus, *The Chronicle of Henry of Livonia*, Bk. 1, ch. I, n. 8

[143] Henricus Lettus, *The Chronicle of Henry of Livonia*, Bk. 3, ch. VII, n. 39

[144] Simon Franklin and Jonathan Shepard, *The Emergence of Rus, 750–1200* (New York: Longman, 1996); Janet Martin, *Medieval Russia, 980–1584* (Cambridge: Cambridge University Press, 1996).

[145] Marcus Wheeler, *The Oxford Russian-English Dictionary*, 2nd ed. (Oxford: Oxford University Press, 1992), 284.

[146] *The Kingdom of Rus* (Leeds: Arc Humanities Press, 2017).

as "king," as Henry of Livonia originally used. So, why is this not reflected in the scholarship or in translations?

As is often the case, there are several reasons for why *kniaz'* is translated as prince. One is due to the vagaries of the denotation and connotation of "king." Another is historical practice. Those two will be dealt with sequentially here. The first issue does not have anything specific to do with the word *kniaz'*, or really the word prince, but primarily with the word "king." The third of the Henry of Livonia quotations above, regarding "Russian kings" illustrates the problem well. There were many people in Rus who bore the title king. Henry did not have a problem with this. Similarly, Abbot Wilhelm, writing around the same time as Henry of Livonia, noted that Queen Sophia of Denmark was born to the "king of the Rusians, for they have many kings there."[147] Wilhelm, like Henry, does not include a statement of judgment when he notes the multiple kings, he is simply sharing information and wants to clarify for his audience. For modern peoples, though, multiple kings is an oxymoron. King equals monarch, and monarch is, literally, a sole ruler, thus there can be only one.[148] The idea that in Rus there were multiple kings then immediately disqualifies the ruler from having the title of king, despite the fact that this was the title which they were given in multiple Latin sources (*rex*) and Scandinavian sources (*konungr*); and even despite the shared etymology of *kniaz'* with *konungr* and even with king. It is much more common in modern medieval history writing to give the title of king to a sole ruler, such as a king of England. Even when said sole ruler, also had other kings subordinate to him whether that be Alfred the Great or Henry II. There, historians are willing to make an exception due to the early Middle Ages, or to anticipatory association.[149] The mindset which, I would suggest, developed as part of the Enlightenment has situated within moderns a hierarchical worldview and a need for structure, especially in government, that was absent for much of the middle ages. Another place to see this same phenomenon is in coins. Medieval numismatics is a robust field, and coin collections have been carefully curated at universities and institutions such as Dumbarton Oaks. To take just one figure, the mid-eleventh-century Eudokia Makrembolitsa as an example, we can see her on multiple coins in the DO collection. She appears with her husband, Romanus IV Diogenes on a coin

[147] "Wilhelmi Abbatis Genealogia Regum Danorum," in *Scriptores minores historiae danicae medii ævi*, vol. 1 of 2, ed. M. C. L. Getz (Copenhagen: I Kommission hos G. E. C. Gad, 1917), 184.

[148] *Shorter Oxford English Dictionary*, vol. 1: A-M (Oxford: Oxford University Press, 2007 [6th ed.]), 1506.

[149] C. Warren Hollister, "Normandy, France and the Anglo-Norman Regnum," *Speculum* 51:2 (1976): 202–242.

during their rule and yet the coin is labeled simply as "Nomisma tetarteron of Romanos IV Diogenes (1068-1071)" with no mention of Eudokia (Figure 7).[150]

Eudokia's presence was essential for Romanos IV because it was via her authority as the widow of Constantine X and regent for their sons, that he was allowed to claim royal authority at all. The complexity of the situation can be clearly seen on other coins and seals wherein Eudokia and her sons with Constantine X appear with Romanos IV regularly.[151] The DO collection does include Eudokia in its catalog, "Nomisma histamenon of Eudokia Makrembolitissa (1067)" (Figure 8).[152]

Yet, this coin does not simply depict Eudokia, but her children with Constantine X as well. Eudokia may have been ruling, but her rule was inextricable from that of her children for whom she acted as regent. It was on their behalf that she married Romanos IV to provide a protector for their legacy, even while he was accused of acting against them. The corulership on both of these coins was done on purpose to demonstrate visually to the people of the Roman Empire who their rulers were. The images included connectivity with

Figure 7 Nomisma tetarteron of Romanos IV Diogenes (1068-1071) (Dumbarton Oaks Collection BZC.1948.17.3232)

[150] BZC.1948.17.3232.

[151] www.doaks.org/resources/online-exhibits/gods-regents-on-earth-a-thousand-years-of-byzantine-imperial-seals/rulers-of-byzantium/bzs.1958.106.600.

[152] BZC.1948.17.3221.

Figure 8 Nomisma histamenon of Eudokia Makrembolitissa (1067) (Dumbarton Oaks Collection BZC.1948.17.3221)

the past ruler via Eudokia and via her sons, connections which were essential for claims of current power. But for moderns this level of complication does not easily fit into our hierarchical categorization of rule. The Roman Empire is ruled by an emperor; singular. Thus, we need to be able to choose an emperor to occupy that position, from the many given to us by our source materials.

All of which is highly relevant to the situation in regard to Rus. Multiple rulers with the same title at the same time created the idea that there was no political centralization and hierarchy with a king at the top of a pyramid. Thus, there could be no king and the translation for the rulers of Rus needed to be something of which there could be many, prince or duke (the latter more common before the twentieth century) fit the bill nicely. It is worth emphasizing that the issue in regard to a plurality of rulers is not centered on Rus, but on our modern perceptions of rule and corulership. By exploring what we think we know, perhaps we can gain a better understanding of the ways that medieval peoples approached their own rulership.[153]

The multiplicity of rulers with the same title was one problem, but there is also the problem of historical translation which needs discussion. Rus was connected into the medieval European world and its rulers appear in Latin, Old Norse, and Greek sources. But it was not until the early modern period that English travelers, writing in English, reached the area and began writing about

[153] The topic of corulership is discussed more in *Rulers and Rulership in the Arc of Medieval Europe* (New York: Routledge, 2023), 58–96.

the polities which they found there. Queen Elizabeth of England had ties with the court of Ivan IV of Moscow and his son Feodor. One of her most famous ambassadors was Giles Fletcher who traveled to Muscovy in 1588 and wrote about the experience a few years later in a work entitled "Of the Russe Commonwealth: or, Maner of Governement by the Russe emperour (commonly called the Emperour of Moskovia) with the manners and fashions of the people of that Countrey."[154] The full title, in properly elaborate Elizabethan form, denotes the subject and is important for why Fletcher is used here. Fletcher approached Muscovy as an empire, with an emperor. When he wrote about the nobility, who served under the emperor, he categorized them as he saw them in the late sixteenth century, but also through the inevitable lens of his own experience. Thus, he says, "The degrees of persons or estates of Russia (besides the soveraigne state or emperor himselfe), are these in their order."[155] The first and fourth are the most important orders for our purposes, and Fletcher's text will be quoted here at length:

> The nobility, which is of four sortes. Whereof the chiefs for birth, authoritie, and revenue are called the *udelney knazey*, that is, the exempted or priviledged dukes . . . The fourth and lowest degree of nobilitie with them is of such as beare the name of *knazey* or dukes, but come of the younger brothers of those chiefe houses, through many descents, and have no inheritance of their owne, save the bare name or title of duke onely.[156]

Fletcher notes the Russian names for the titles "*udelney knazey*" and "*knazey*" and also renders both of them into English as "dukes." Fletcher's diagram of the political pyramid is not inaccurate. He has an excellent grasp of the various families which make up the ranks, their status both real and imagined in the empire, and how they all fit together. However, the societal ranks as existent at the end of the sixteenth century do not necessarily fit the model of the Middle Ages. Fletcher was describing a system with an emperor at the top of the political hierarchy, and the various *kniazia*, dukes in his translation, were subordinate to that emperor. They would not be kings in any fashion in the sixteenth century. Fletcher's work, and other travel accounts of this period, created the basis for translation of ideas and concepts from Russian into English which lasts to this day; and yet still describe only the sixteenth century in particular. Fletcher himself seems to have understood the problem of change

---

154 Giles Fletcher, "Of the Russe Commonwealth: Or, Maner of Governement by the Russe emperour (commonly called the Emperour of Moskovia) with the manners and fashions of the people of that Countrey," in *Russia at the Close of the Sixteenth Century*, ed. Edward A. Bond (London: Hakluyt Society, 1856), 1–152.

155 Fletcher, "Of the Russe Commonwealth," Ch. IX, p. 32.

156 Fletcher, "Of the Russe Commonwealth," Ch. IX, p. 32, 38.

over time in titles, as he notes that in the eleventh century there was "the Russe king Vlademir, sirnamed Jaruslave, that married the daughter of Harald king of England."[157] This Volodimer was actually the son of Vsevolod who was himself the son of Iaroslav, but such a mistake is easy to make several hundred years after the fact. Volodimer Vsevolodich "Monomakh" did marry Gyða Haroldsdottir and they had a son named Magnus, who was called "Harald" in Scandinavian sources, after his maternal grandfather.[158] All of this is fascinating in that Fletcher knew the dynastic marriage connecting Rus to Anglo-Saxon England, but even more interesting is that Fletcher called Volodimer a king. His knowledge of sixteenth-century Muscovy also included the knowledge that in the eleventh century, the Rusian ruler was a king, even if he had the same title, *kniaz'*, as those whom Fletcher termed dukes. This institutional knowledge and willingness to acknowledge change over time has been missed, and the direct translation of *kniaz'* as duke has taken hold as the normative translation into English. Something which even Fletcher would have understood was not accurate for medieval Europe.

Governance in Rus

Governance and Rus are rarely seen in the same sentence, or even paragraph, in most of the secondary literature. The textbook discussion of Rus is one marred by internecine warfare, while the medieval polity is typically used as a failed stand-in for later, centralized, Muscovite governance.[159] However, if we set aside the received wisdom about a plurality of rulers with the same title being a problem, and decentralized rule being a problem (two omnipresent concerns in the scholarship on medieval studies), it is possible to return to the primary sources and look at the ways in which the polity of Rus was ruled.[160] This of course requires a brief note about those primary sources.

---

[157] Fletcher, "Of the Russe Commonwealth," Ch. III, p. 18.

[158] Christian Raffensperger, *Ties of Kinship: Genealogy and Dynastic Marriage in Kyivan Rus'* (Cambridge, MA: Harvard Ukrainian Research Institute, 2016), 62–63.

[159] "The reigns of Iziaslav, Sviatoslav, and Vsevolod, the last of whom died in 1093, as well as that of Iziaslav's son Sviatopolk, who succeeded Vsevolod and ruled until his death in 1113, present a frightening record of virtually constant civil wars which failed to resolve with any degree of permanence the problem of political power in Kievan Russia." Nicholas V. Riasanovsky, *A History of Russia* 5th ed. (New York, Oxford: Oxford University Press, 1993), 33; "Rus Was Not at First a Unified Polity but a Mafia-Like Network of Merchants and Warlords," *Russia's Empire*, ed. Valerie A. Kivelson and Ronald Grigor Suny (Oxford: Oxford University Press, 2017), 17.

[160] This idea of rulership is elaborated in "Kyivan Rus: A Complicated Kingdom," in *How Medieval Europe was Ruled*, ed. Christian Raffensperger (New York: Routledge, 2023), 176–190.

The main source for Rusian history of this period is the *Povest' vremennykh let* (PVL) which was commissioned by the ruling clan, and largely favors the line of Vsevolod Iaroslavich.[161] It was written or compiled at the end of the eleventh and beginning of the twelfth centuries, most likely in or around Kyiv. The narrative focus of this chronicle is almost entirely about the ruling clan of Rus, and seldom discusses town affairs that are not relevant to its main subject. Another early source is the chronicle from Novgorod. This chronicle places Novgorod at the center. The ruling clan is included when relevant to the city, but it also records information about the mayors, military leaders, local priests and bishops, and much more that is not seen in the PVL. A third early source are the laws created by Iaroslav Volodimerich and his children in the eleventh century, though extant only from a later period. The laws are about minutiae that are almost entirely absent from the chronicle sources. They detail the existence of numerous governmental positions, discuss women, slaves, and animals, and record the importance of people not of the ruling clan. It is largely these three sources, with the addition of some archaeological finds, which will be woven together to present a picture of the governance of Rus.

Rus was ruled from Kyiv on the Dnieper River. The breadth of the polity changed over time, but from the time of Oleg's conquest of the city in the late ninth century, we can see that this was the case. The treaty which he made with the Roman Emperors, Leo and Alexander, is between them and a series of envoys (discussed in Section 1) who were "sent by Oleg, great king of Rus and from all those under his hand."[162] Oleg is primary here, and it is clear that he rules over the others who sent envoys as well as that he ruled Rus. Following the treaty, the PVL records that the envoys returned to Kyiv and told Oleg of what had been agreed and, "Oleg lived at peace with all countries and ruled in Kyiv."[163] Oleg was the ruler of Rus and ruler of Kyiv; as far as the chronicle is concerned the two positions are coterminous. The same formula is repeated in the treaty between the Romans and Oleg's successor Igor in the mid-tenth century, down to the phrase that he lived at peace with all countries and ruled in Kyiv.[164] When Volodimer Sviatoslavich "began to rule alone in Kyiv" in 980, he sat his uncle Dobrynia in Novgorod to rule the second city of the polity on his behalf.[165] In 988, the PVL records that Volodimer assigned his sons, who were presumably of age, to rule various towns and cities of Rus: "He placed Iaroslav over Novgorod, Boris over Rostov, Gleb over Murom, Sviatoslav over Dereva,

[161] *The Old Rus' Kievan and Galician-Volhynian Chronicles*, xx. [162] PVL, s.a. 912.

[163] PVL, s.a. 912. As an interesting note, the Old Slavonic phrase here is къняжа въ Кыевѣ where the initial word is the conjugated verb k"niazha, derived from the noun *kniaz'*. And yet the phrase is never translated as Oleg "princed" from Kyiv.

[164] PVL, s.a. 941. [165] PVL, s.a. 980.

Vsevolod over Vladimir, and Mstislav over Tmutorokan."[166] The ability to place subordinate rulers in the towns of Rus is indicative of the position of the ruler of Kyiv as the ruler of Rus as a whole. In the case of Volodimer he was not only ruler of Kyiv, but also *pater familias*, which would set a precedent for the ruler to manage the kingdom and the clan, which were in some ways coterminous. After Volodimer's death, the primacy of Kyiv was challenged by a conflict between his sons Iaroslav and Mstislav. As noted in 988, Iaroslav ruled in Novgorod, and was most likely the eldest son of Volodimer, though any specifics about this are complicated given that it was Iaroslav's line, not those of his rivals, which commissioned the PVL. Mstislav ruled in Tmutorokan, a city in the south of Rus, along the Black Sea, separated from the bulk of Rus by the steppe. By 1019, Iaroslav had settled in Kyiv, and by 1021 was keeping the peace throughout Rus after a raid by a member of the clan on Novgorod.[167] However, in 1023, the PVL records laconically that "Mstislav went against Iaroslav with Kazars and Kasogians."[168] The conflict between the two was settled in 1026 when they divided Rus into two, along the Dnieper River, with Iaroslav's capital at Kyiv, ruling the right bank (western side), and Mstislav's at Chernigov, ruling the left bank (eastern side).[169] Rus was now two polities rather than one, but the two rulers were brothers, members of the same ruling clan, and continued to cooperate with each other against foreign opponents.[170] The split in Rus lasted only until Mstislav's death in 1036, his son had predeceased him, and at that time Iaroslav once again became the "sole ruler" in Rus.[171] Perhaps to affirm that, the very next sentence in the PVL has Iaroslav going to Novgorod where he named his son Volodimer as the ruler, and appointed Zhidiata as bishop; demonstrating his rights as ruler over all of Rus to appoint subordinate rulers. Even as Rus, and the ruling clan, grew, this remained a privilege of the ruler of Kyiv, such as in 1078 when Vsevolod Iaroslavich assumed the throne of Kyiv and held "all power in Rus" he appointed subordinate rulers and rearranged some of the existing property.[172] Thus, though we see members of the ruling clan in various cities and towns of Rus in this period with the same title, *kniaz'*, it is clear from the Rusian sources that the ruler of Kyiv was the ruler of Rus. This is reflected in the foreign sources as well, where he is referred to not as the ruler of Kyiv, but as the ruler *(rex)* of the Rusians.[173]

---

[166] PVL, s.a. 988. This is the second assignment of towns which took place following Vysheslav's death. Both are listed in this entry, one after the other.

[167] PVL, s.a. 1019, 1021. [168] PVL, s.a. 1023. [169] PVL, s.a. 1026.

[170] For instance, in taking advantage of succession difficulties in Poland, when they took back territory in 1031. PVL, s.a. 1031.

[171] PVL, s.a. 1036. [172] PVL, s.a. 1078.

[173] *Annalista Saxo*, in *Monumenta Germaniae Historica: Scriptores* 6 (Hannover: Impensis Bibliopolii Avlici Hahniani, 1844): s.a. 1089, when referring to the aforementioned Vsevolod.

While the ruler of Kyiv was the ruler of Rus as a whole, this did not require him to be everywhere in Rus at once. He had subordinates who ruled in the various towns and paid him tribute from their regions.[174] Such an arrangement was not at all unusual. The king of the Franks operated the same way at this time and may have held even less direct power over his subordinates than the Rusian ruler did.[175] The ruler of Kyiv, like other rulers in Rus, was itinerant to some degree and when they traveled, they traveled with their families.[176] Though they did have a capital and did hold court there; for instance, Volodimer Sviatoslavich was said to hold a feast each Sunday at his court to which he invited his "boyars, retinue, centurions and decurions" whether he was there or not.[177] Each of these enumerated positions is interesting in its own right and worthy of discussion. Their grouping together here suggests that Volodimer was interested in keeping his power base, largely military men, happy. The first group are the boyars, a word that is often left untranslated into English as there is a strong perception that this word is understood already. Here we can return to Giles Fletcher who says that the second "Degree of nobility is of the *Boiarens*. These are such as the emperour honoureth (besides their nobility) with the title of counsellers."[178] In early modern Muscovy, boyar was a defined rank, as Fletcher notes. But this is not necessarily the case in medieval Rus, despite the use of the same, or similar word, at the time – a problem which has already been encountered. Tatiana Vilkul has analyzed the use of this word in Rusian chronicles and notes two things of interest here.[179] The first is that the word is archaic in this period and is rarely used in the sources. The second is that the word does not seem to have a permanent meaning. For instance, in the twelfth-century *Kyivan Chronicle*, "the same group consisting of Raguilo, Michal and Zavid is differently described three times as a retinue (*druzhina*), boyars and men (*muzhi*)."[180] The author of the chronicle seems to have been, drawing on other of Vilkul's examples as well, using a diversity of words, thesaurus-like, to talk about the same group of people in an extended narrative sequence. Vilkul's interpretation runs counter to what many scholars have suggested in the past,

[174] Iaroslav's failure to provide such tribute was the *casus belli* for Volodimer's war against him. PVL, s.a. 1014.

[175] R. van Caenegem, "Government, Law and Society," in *The Cambridge History of Medieval Political Thought, c. 350-1450*, ed. J. H. Burns (Cambridge: Cambridge University Press, 1988), 176.

[176] *Name Unknown: The Life of a Rusian Queen* (New York: Routledge, 2023), 15–16.

[177] PVL, s.a. 996

[178] Fletcher, "Of the Russe Commonwealth," Ch. IX, p. 36.

[179] Tatiana Vilkul, "People and Boyars in the Old Russian Chronicles of the 11th–13th Centuries: Narrative Modelling of Social Identities," in *Imagined Communities: Constructing Collective Identities in Medieval Europe*, ed. Andrzej Pleszczyński, Joanna Sobiesiak, Michał Tomaszek, Przemysław Tyszka (Leiden and Boston: Brill, 2018), 179–203.

[180] Vilkul, "People and Boyars in the Old Russian Chronicles," 186.

including Petr Stefanovich's monograph on the topic which creates a hierarchical organization from the chronicle material with boyars immediately subordinate to the *kniaz'*, and over the guards.[181] Such a hierarchy is a consequence of our post-Enlightenment thinking. Vilkul's analysis seems to be correct, and the world of labels is more one of sand than bedrock. Thus, the boyars can be seen as nobles, but they do not need to have a specific rank at court.

The other three groups listed are perhaps easier to codify as they are all explicitly military men, though given Vilkul's example of Raguilo, Michal and Zavid as boyars and a warband (*druzhina*), it could perhaps be more complicated still. The first group are identified here as a retinue, though this word can also be translated as guards.[182] The name for them is the noun form of the place where the banquets were held at the court, and thus retinue, or even courtiers, seems to be an accurate description. The same group is referenced in the Russkaia Pravda, the earliest Rusian law code, where the very first law includes them as a protected group.[183] This group is also present in Novgorod, as seen in 1014 when Iaroslav's retinue there is given 1,000 grivnas per year.[184] The following two groups were listed here as "centurions" and "decurions" as one imagines these are familiar terms to historians. The Old Slavonic versions carry the same meanings of commander of 100 and commander of 10. The *sotnik*, or centurion, is also mentioned in the Novgorod chronicle, for the first time in 1118.[185] This commander is mentioned regularly in the "Statute of the Novgorod Prince Vsevolod" from the 1130s. In particular, the law specifies that Vsevold, the ruler of Novgorod at the time, "summoned ten hundred-men" along with other important city officials, including his wife, to assign privileges relating to the markets.[186] The hundredmen have specific tasks recorded in the laws, including supervising the Church of Holy Sophia alongside the archbishop, and acting as surety for the ruler's descendants to ensure that they comply with the laws as laid out here.[187] They are also given one-third of the

---

181 P. S. Stefanovich, *Boiare, otroki, druzhiny: Voenno-politicheskaia elita Rusi v X-XI vekakh* (Moscow: Indrik, 2012). See for example, the charts on 568 and 569, though of course also the text beginning at 359.

182 *Slovar' russkogo iazyka, X-XVII vv.* Vol. 4 (G-D) (Moscow: Nauka, 1977), 136–137.

183 "The Russkaia Pravda: The Short Redaction (Academy Copy)" transl. Daniel Kaiser in *The Laws of Rus' – Tenth to Fifteenth Centuries*, transl. and ed. Daniel H. Kaiser (Salt Lake City, Utah: Charles Schlacks Jr., 1992): art. 1, p 15.

184 PVL, s.a. 1014. 185 NPL, s.a. 1118. Though it also appears twice more, in 1195 and 1216.

186 "Statute of the Novgorod Prince Vsevolod [1135–37] on Church Courts, [Church] People, and Trade Measures," transl. Daniel Kaiser in *The Laws of Rus' – Tenth to Fifteenth Centuries*, transl. And ed. Daniel H. Kaiser (Salt Lake City, Utah: Charles Schlacks Jr., 1992): art. 4, pp. 59–60.

187 "Statute of the Novgorod Prince Vsevolod," art. 6, p. 60; art. 23, p. 62.

property of any crooked merchants who are found to have faulty scales.[188] The decurion, the leader of ten men, appears in the PVL, as well as in the same "Statute of the Novgorod Prince Vsevolod" where the hundredmen were included. This position may be an instance of appropriation from the Roman Empire as the article says, "Lo we have found in the Greek nomocanon that a ruler is not to hold court [over church people . . .]" nor should any of his staff, including his commanders of ten men.[189] The lack of references to this group make it a bit suspect, especially in the context of the Greek nomocanon, but it would make some level of military sense to have leaders of ten men, when there also exist leaders of 100 men, and leaders of 1,000 men.

Leaders of 1,000 men seem to have been a regular feature of the towns of Rus, though they only appear one time in the PVL. The "Expanded Redaction" of the Rusian law code contains an article stating that Volodimer Vsevolodich created new laws after having consulted with "Ratibor the Kyivan commander of 1000, Prokopia the Belgorod commander of 1000, Stanislav the Pereiaslav commander of 1000" and several other individuals.[190] Ratibor appears twice in the PVL, as a close advisor to Vsevolod Iaroslavich and then to his son Volodimer Monomakh.[191] Ratibor is not a member of the ruling clan, but he does hold important positions and has wealth. In 1079, Vsevolod appoints him as the *posadnik* or mayor of Tmutorokan, after engineering a rival's removal.[192] Ratibor appears later living in Pereiaslavl and working for Volodimer Monomakh, on whose behalf he houses and then kills a Polovtsian hostage.[193] At this time he was not the Kyivan commander of a 1000, but it is possible that he was the commander of 1000 for Pereiaslavl. The Kyivan commander of 1000 was Ian Vyshatich who appears regularly in the PVL as a soldier working for Iaroslav and his sons, though he is only once described with the title of commander of 1000.[194] The continuity of this position is difficult to track, but in both cases mentioned here, Ratibor and Ian, we see familial connections to power. Ian's father, Vyshata, was a military leader in Novgorod who led Volodimer Iaroslavich's failed 1043 assault on Constantinople, and later assisted his son Rostislav in seizing the city of Tmutorokan.[195] While Foma Ratiborich, assumedly Ratibor's son given the onomastic evidence, is listed in 1121 as the mayor of Cherven, a border town with the Poles.[196] In that year, he repels an attack by Iaroslav Sviatopolchich and the Poles; indicative of his serving Volodimer Monomakh and his family, as his father had. The position of commander of 1000 occurs regularly in the Novgorod

[188] "Statute of the Novgorod Prince Vsevolod," art. 15, p. 61.

[189] "Statute of the Novgorod Prince Vsevolod," art. 3, p. 60.

[190] "The Russkaia Pravda: The Expanded Redaction (Trinity Copy)," transl. Daniel Kaiser in *The Laws of Rus' – Tenth to Fifteenth Centuries*, transl. and ed. Daniel H. Kaiser (Salt Lake City, Utah: Charles Schlacks Jr., 1992): art. 55, p. 26.

[191] PVL, s.a. 1079, 1095. [192] PVL, s.a. 1079. [193] PVL, s.a. 1095. [194] PVL, s.a. 1089.

[195] PVL, s.a. 1043, 1064. [196] Kievan Chronicle, s.a. 1121.

chronicle record beginning with Miloneg, in 1191, erecting a church.[197] Though we do not have information about who appointed him, he is clearly someone important given that he had the money to erect a church, which the archbishop consecrated in that year. Extant Novgorodian treaties of the thirteenth and early fourteenth centuries begin with a listing of the important figures of Novgorod who were present, and each of them includes a commander of 1000.[198] It seems likely that this figure is a major military figure in each of the cities given the evidence that we have.

Another official who appears quite often, and in numerous places, is the mayor or *posadnik* in Old Slavonic. The position of mayor is most often associated with Novgorod and there appear numerous officials with that title in the Novgorod chronicles. One of those mayors even has a daughter marry Mstislav Volodimerich before he became king of Rus – a rarity among the interkingdom dynastic marriages which were frequent at this time and indicative of the power of the mayoral office and Novgorod. The Novgorodian *posadniki* have been studied extensively, though typically with the same quest for hierarchical organization discussed earlier.[199] These officials appear regularly in the Novgorodian chronicles after 1117 when the title first appears in Novgorod with the death of Dobrynia.[200] It is quite interesting that the first named *posadnik* of Novgorod coincides with the uncle of Volodimer Sviatoslavich whom he assigned as posadnik of the city in the PVL in 980.[201] In 1116, the year before Dobrynia's death is recorded, a *posadnik* for Ladoga, a town near Novgorod, is mentioned as having laid the first stone foundations.[202] In 1132, a *posadnik* for Pskov is mentioned, and (as discussed earlier), Foma Ratiborich was *posadnik* of Cherven in 1121.[203] Thus, we see this office exist elsewhere than just Novgorod. The process of how one became a mayor was unknown, though the dominant train of thought was laid down by V.L. Ianin who suggested that they were chosen by the *veche* at the direction of the boyars.[204] What the primary sources provide is more complicated. In the

---

197 NPL, s.a. 1191.

198 "The First Treaty of Novgorod with Tver' Grand Prince Iaroslav Iaroslavich [1230–71], ca. 1264-65," transl. Daniel Kaiser in *The Laws of Rus' – Tenth to Fifteenth Centuries*, transl. And ed. Daniel H. Kaiser (Salt Lake City, Utah: Charles Schlacks Jr., 1992), 67; "Treaty of Novgorod with Tver' Grand Prince Mikhail Iaroslavich [1271–1318], 1304–5," transl. Daniel Kaiser in *The Laws of Rus' – Tenth to Fifteenth Centuries*, transl. and ed. Daniel H. Kaiser (Salt Lake City, Utah: Charles Schlacks Jr., 1992), 69.

199 V. L. Ianin, *Novgorodskie posadniki* (Moscow: Izdatel'stvo Moskovskogo universiteta, 1962).

200 NPL, s.a. 1117. 201 PVL, s.a. 980. 202 NPL, s.a. 1116.

203 NPL, s.a. 1132; Kievan Chronicle, s.a. 1121.

204 For a contestation of this and the entire concept of the veche see Jonas Granberg, *Veche in the Chronicles of Medieval Rus: A Study of Functions and Terminology* (Göteborg: Göteborg University, 2004).

twelfth century, the Novgorod chronicle says that X "became *posadnik*," or "was appointed" as *posadnik*, and *posadniki* could also be removed by unnamed forces, "the Novgorodians" or by the Novgorodian ruler.[205] It can be assumed that the mayors had administrative functions, as they do have their own seals, but we do not have explicit documentation of what those functions were.[206] Sometimes *posadniki* come from elsewhere to Novgorod, though it is unclear if they were originally Novgorodians, and we see them leave as ambassadors or military leaders, though one could speculate that these are anecdotal examples. Regardless of the specifics, the *posadnik* as mayor was an important, if undefined for us, role in Rusian governance.

The positions discussed thus far typically appear in chronicle sources which means that there is often some explication, even if not much, of their role. The Rusian law code contains numerous governmental positions whose function can only be guessed at as they rarely, if ever, appear in any other source. In article 1 of the Russkaia Pravda a list of figures is provided which includes, "a member of the retinue, merchant, *iabetnik*, guard."[207] The retinue has been discussed already and merchants are clear, but the *iabetnik* and guard are new categories. Guard, swordsman literally (*mechnik*), is a commonplace in the law codes and it should not surprise us that guards were a staple of medieval governance, though it is nice to have that confirmed.[208] *Iabetnik* has been translated as "agent" and as "bailiff," but the precise functions are simply not known.[209] Other articles of the law code add additional authority figures including the *ognishchanin, podiezdnoi, tivun, koniukh stary, starosta,* and *virnik*.[210] George Vernadsky, in his book on *Kievan Russia*, used these articles to create a hierarchy which draws on later sources related to boyar courts.[211] This is typical, and is an attempt to make sense of early sources with recourse to later ones. Just looking at the law code, which provides the source for these titles, the evidence of what they do is very thin. *Ognishchanin* is most likely a steward, and appears quite often in the laws. Vernadsky suggests that he was in charge of the farms, given what is

---

205 All examples drawn from the NPL in the twelfth century.

206 Ianin discusses the seals in his *Novgorodskie posadniki,* and several appear in his seal collection. *Aktovye pechati drevnei rusi X-XV vv.* tom 1 of 3: Pechati X-nachala XIII v., ed. V. L. Ianin (Moscow: Nauka, 1970).

207 "The Russkaia Pravda: The Short Redaction (Academy Copy)," art. 1 p. 15.

208 George Vernadsky calls this terminology into question and suggests "sheriff" for mechnik and an alternate derivation of the word. *Medieval Russian Laws*, transl. George Vernadsky (New York: Oxford University Press, 1947), 26n1.

209 Vernadsky compares it to a Swedish position, which is why he chooses agent. *Medieval Russian Laws*, 26n1. Kaiser uses bailiff. "The Russkaia Pravda: The Short Redaction (Academy Copy)," art. 1 p. 15.

210 "The Russkaia Pravda: The Short Redaction (Academy Copy)," art. 19–24, 33, 41–42; pp. 17–19.

211 George Vernadsky, *Kievan Russia* (New Haven: Yale University Press, 1948), 138.

recorded in article 21, though that article only notes his murder near a barn.[212] *Podiezdnoi* has been translated as messenger, adjutant and a collector of fines, though it rarely appears again in the laws. *Tivun* is a term that occurs with some regularity and may be derived from the Old Norse word for "servant."[213] The next two figures seem to be clear in that the *koniukh stary* is clearly the senior horseman, or stablemaster, and he is particularly tied to the ruler of Kyiv in article 23 with relation to the time that "the residents of Dorogobuzh killed his [Iziaslav's] stablemaster."[214] *Starosta* literally means elder, but in context it is the elder of the fields.[215] *Virnik* is one of the most interesting positions and is regularly translated as "bloodwite collector." This position, who also later had an assistant, would collect the fees people were required to pay for crimes. The division of the fine is articulated in article 41 and clearly subordinates the bloodwite collector to the ruler.[216] The bloodwite collector is also someone who is provided with provisions to help them in their job as they travel to collect fees.[217] Though just a glimpse is given via the law codes, the existence of these positions pulls back the curtain slightly in terms of looking at Rusian governance. Sadly, there is little additional information which would allow us to create a structured Rusian government from the fragments which remain extant.

The chronicles provide a narrative of people and events, though largely just the elites. The law codes provide a great deal of additional information about the names of positions, and some about their roles. What is missing is the administrative communication that makes up the fabric of governance which would help explain how all of the various positions discussed here interacted with one another. France, though having some of the same governmental issues at this time, has a charter record that is largely unmatched in western Europe.[218] Rus, on the other hand, has one of the worst preservation records for written material. 300 manuscript books or fragments exist from prior to 1300 in Rus, only twenty-three of which are from the eleventh century.[219] The majority of that 300 are religious documents, which do not often help shed light on the governmental picture within Rus. It is possible that the scarcity is due to a preservation issue rather than a lack of created documents. Writing did exist in ways that

[212] "The Russkaia Pravda: The Short Redaction (Academy Copy)," art. 21, p. 17; *Medieval Russian Laws*, 30n19.

[213] *Medieval Russian Laws*, 31n22.

[214] "The Russkaia Pravda: The Short Redaction (Academy Copy)," art. 23, p. 17.

[215] "The Russkaia Pravda: The Short Redaction (Academy Copy)," art. 24, p. 17.

[216] "The Russkaia Pravda: The Short Redaction (Academy Copy)," art. 41, p. 18.

[217] "The Russkaia Pravda: The Short Redaction (Academy Copy)," art. 42, pp. 18–19.

[218] Which provides the basis for numerous monographs, such as Amy Livingstone, *Out of Love for My Kin: Aristocratic Family Life in the Lands of the Loire, 1000–1200* (Cornell: Cornell University Press, 2010).

[219] Franklin, *Writing, Society and Culture in Early Rus'*, 23.

make it seem somewhat casual. Birch bark documents excavated in Novgorod have become well known in scholarly circles, often due to the playful illustrations which accompany things such as alphabet sets (see Figure 9 – where a boat is drawn).

When Simon Franklin wrote his study of writing in Rus over 20 years ago, he was able to dismiss the circa 500 birch bark documents from before 1300 as not indicative of widespread literacy.[220] Since that time, though, excavations and publications have continued and the number of birch bark documents has grown steadily with an ever increasing peak in the second half of the twelfth century.[221] The documents are also not just from Novgorord, though the intensive excavation there over the last seventy years has certainly supplied the vast majority. Excavations have also unearthed birchbark documents from Starja Russa, Smolensk, Moscow, Pskov, Tver, Riazan, Mstislavl (Belarus), Vitebsk (Belarus), and Zvenigorod Galickij (Ukraine).[222] As one can see from the list, there is a wide swath of territory covered by the finds, and modern Ukraine, thus the heartland of medieval Rus, is largely unrepresented. It is possible that no birchbark documents exist from there given soil conditions, however, they could have been destroyed, or not found as yet.[223] Writing also exists as graffiti in churches and even carved into the walls of Kyiv.[224] Sometimes what is written is a doodle or drawing, as of a boar hunt, others recognize the arrival of a member of the ruling clan, and some seem to have the character of notarized documents.[225] Such as an inscription from the Holy Sophia church

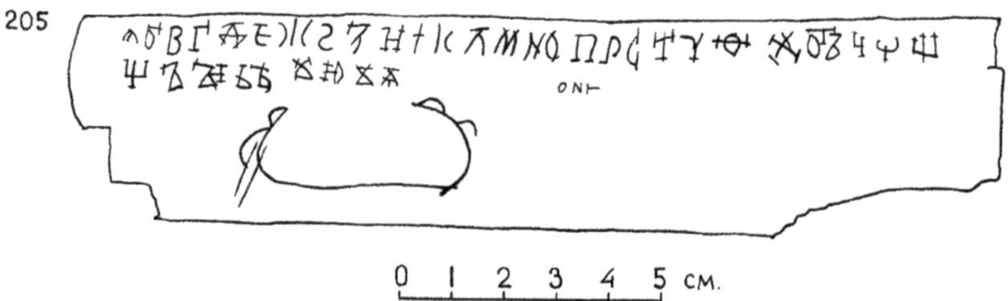

Figure 9 Birchbark letter no. 205

[220] Franklin, *Writing, Society and Culture in Early Rus'*, 38–40.

[221] Jos. Schaeken, "Comments on birchbark documents found in the twenty-first century: Zamechaniia k berestniam gramotam, naidennym v XXI veke," *Russian Linguistics* 41 (2017): 123–149, especially Figure 1, p. 125.

[222] Schaeken, "Comments on birchbark documents," 125–126.

[223] The current Russo-Ukraine war makes it unlikely that excavations will take place at any time in Ukraine in the near future.

[224] S. A. Vysotskii, *Kievskie graffiti XI-XVII vv.* (Kiev: Naukova Dumka, 1985); Franklin, *Writing, Society and Culture in Early Rus'*, 71–74.

[225] Vysotskii, *Kievskie graffiti*, 12–13.

in Kyiv which says, "Vsevolod's queen . . . purchased Boian's land . . . " and contains witness information, as well as the price.[226] These too could be seen as incidental, except that new inscriptions have been discovered as far as the Abbey of St. Gilles in France.[227] Additionally, the style of writing of the graffiti in Rus seems to be uniquely Rusian and reflect a style divorced from that of the copyists who wrote many of the manuscripts.[228]

Even without the discovery of a massive tranche of documents, evidence exists that there could be more documents than we have extant. The Roman-Rusian treaties inserted into the PVL say that the Rusian ruler must provide authentication seals for his ambassadors and merchants.[229] The brief 971 treaty with Sviatoslav concludes with, "which we have written on this parchment and sealed with our seals."[230] While no seals are extant for Oleg or Igor, Sviatoslav does have extant seals, thus though the "parchment" copy is not extant, perhaps the seals are, or at least some seals of his.[231] The sigillographic record for Rus is nowhere near the 50,000 medieval French seals, but a decent size catalog exists and has been documented by V. L. Ianin.[232] Seals exist for rulers of Kyiv and other cities; for women such as Christina, wife of Mstislav Volodimerich; for ecclesiastical figures; and for governmental officials such as Ratibor mentioned earlier.[233] Not only do seals exist, but we have seal matrices and most interestingly, signet rings which were designed to seal documents, though most likely in wax rather than lead or gold. Many of these rings are designed and sized for women, indicative of their ability, and need, to seal documents of their own.[234] (See Figure 10.)

Thus, while we have the paraphernalia of a documentary record, we do not have the documentary record itself, and thus the picture of governance in Rus is incomplete. The offices discussed in the chronicle and legal sources can be discussed in detail, but how they all fit together is still a matter of conjecture.

226 M. M. Drobyshcheva, "Graffito No. 25 iz Sofii Kievskoi: Chto my znaem o pokupke 'Boianovoi zemli'?" *Vestnik Permskogo Universiteta* 1 (48) 2020: 130–145.

227 Gordin, "Zametki o palomnicheskikh graffiti abbatstva sen-zhil'," 95–103.

228 Tatiana Nazarenko, "East Slavic Visual Writing: The Inception of Tradition," *Canadian Slavonic Papers / Revue Canadienne des Slavistes* 43:2–3 (2001): 218.

229 PVL, s.a. 945.

230 "The 971 Treaty," transl. Daniel Kaiser in *The Laws of Rus' – Tenth to Fifteenth Centuries*, transl. and ed. Daniel H. Kaiser (Salt Lake City, Utah: Charles Schlacks Jr., 1992): 13.

231 *Aktovye pechati drevnei rusi X-XV vv.* tom 1, 166.

232 Brigitte Bedos-Rezak, "Medieval Women in French Sigillographic Sources," in *Medieval Women and the Sources of Medieval History*, ed. Joel T. Rosenthal (Athens and London: University of Georgia Press, 1990): 1.

233 *Aktovye pechati drevnei rusi*, 166-173 (rulers, male and female), 174–179 (ecclesiastical figures), 180–181 (Ratibor).

234 Ljudmila Pekarska, *Jewellery of Princely Kiev: The Kiev Hoards in the British Museum and the Metropolitan Museum of Art and Related Material*, ed. Barry Ager and Dafydd Kidd (Mainz and London: Verlag des Römisch-Germanischen Zentralmuseums, 2011), 84–92.

Figure 10 Twelfth-century finger ring from Kyiv. (BM 1907.0520.18)

That said, knowing that there was more than just a *kniaz'* or several *kniazia*, that there was a whole array of officials does present a different picture of Rus than the "mafia-like network" which has a grip on the modern scholarly imagination.

4 The Kingdom of Rus in Medieval Europe

The traditional place of Rus in Europe is well known and largely depends upon the image of the Scandinavian-Byzantine trade routes, or the Byzantine Commonwealth. Instead, though brief, this section will focus on the many, many situations wherein Rusians traveled, traded, and engaged in other polities in medieval Europe, and where people from elsewhere came to Rus. Whether through marriage, conflict, trade, or religious travel, Rusians found themselves part of a wider medieval European experience, most especially at the elite level.

Lampert of Hersefeld records that in 1043, "The envoys of the Russians [Rusians – CR] returned home sorrowfully because they brought back a definite rejection of their king's daughter, whom they had hoped to marry to King Henry."[235] The king met the envoys at his favored residence of Goslar, 1,500 kilometers from Kyiv where the Rusian king Iaroslav resided. Several aspects of this situation are worthy of our attention to begin resetting the place of Rus in medieval Europe. Perhaps the most interesting to us is that it was largely uninteresting to the chronicler. Lampert does not begin with a preamble noting

[235] Lampert of Hersfeld, *The Annals of Lampert of Hersfeld*, transl. I. S. Robinson (Manchester: Manchester University Press, 2015), s.a. 1043.

the arrival of people from "an obscure nation, a nation of no account … "[236] Rather, the entry includes the arrival of the duke of Bohemia, and other envoys, including ones from the Hungarians seeking peace. Nothing more needed to be added or expanded upon, no context given, the potential readers knew the players and this was simply a rejected marital alliance. This was not even the only Rusian marital alliance that year as Iaroslav would marry his son Iziaslav to a Polish princess, Gertrude, about whom we know a good deal. Rusians had been sending envoys to the German court for generations by this point. The earliest, and perhaps best known to western medievalists, is the arrival of envoys to the court of Louis the Pious in 839.[237] The Raffelstettin regulations from 906 talk about Rusian merchants and regulates what they can and cannot trade.[238] These connections continue over the century, as we have seen Olga make contact with Otto I for a bishop in approximately 959, and then in 973, Iaropolk sends an envoy to Otto at Quedlinburg.[239] The 973 event is another gathering of numerous envoys, including ones from the medieval Roman Empire, Hungary, Denmark, and elsewhere. All of which is simply to contextualize why the 1043 visit from a Rusian envoy was unremarkable to the chronicler, and, most likely, to the court. The Rusians were a known quantity and had been in contact for well over a century by that point.

The embassy to Goslar to arrange a marriage is often marked as the point at which King Henry I of France became aware of Rus.[240] Whether this is true or not is unknown, though it is certainly possible that knowledge of Rus already existed among the Capetians as Henry himself had previously been married to Henry III's niece Mathilda, and ties between the two polities were consistent. Regardless of how he knew of Rus, in 1049, Henry took action and sent envoys to Rus to arrange a new marriage for himself following Mathilda's death. The "Chronicle of Saint-Pierre-le-Vif of Sens" records that Henry sent Bishops Walter of Melden and Goscelin of Chauney with others to a kingdom on the edge of Greece to ask King Iaroslav of Rus for his daughter's hand in marriage.[241] There is some debate over who led the embassy as Roger, bishop of Chalons, has also been suggested. In a later interpolation into the Psalter of

[236] Cyril Mango, *The Homilies of Photius Patriarch of Constantinople* (Cambridge, MA: Harvard University Press, 1958), IV, p. 98.

[237] *The Annals of St-Bertin*, transl. Janet L. Nelson (New York: Manchester University Press, 1991), s.a. 839.

[238] "Addition Decima: Leges Portorii c.a. 906," in *Monumenta Germaniae Historica. Leges* tom III. (Hannover: Impensis Bibliopolii Avlici Hahniani, 1863), 480–481.

[239] "Lamberti annalium para prior ab O.C. – 1039," in *Monumenta Germaniae Historica: Scriptores* 3 (Hannover: Impensis Bibliopolii Avlici Hahniani, 1839): s.a. 973.

[240] Andrew W. Lewis, *Royal Succession in Capetian France: Studies on Familial Order and the State* (Cambridge, MA: Cambridge University Press, 1981), 45.

[241] Clarius, *Chronique de Sant-Pierre-le-vif de sens, diter de Clarius*, ed. Robert-Henri Bautier and Monique Gilles (Paris: Centre national de la recherche scientifique, 1979), 122.

Odalric, Roger is asked by the titular author to ascertain whether Cherson was in the land of Rus, and whether the miracles of St. Clement were still seen there.[242] Regardless of the composition of delegates, the French sources record a party traveling from Paris to Kyiv, another 1,000 kilometers farther than the Kyiv-Goslar expedition, to arrange a potential marriage. These parties of envoys are of interest, and though we have no details, it is worth imagining a party of Frankish bishops, guards, servants, and so on. travelling across the continent to Kyiv. There is no record of a problem with travel or language recorded, which, by itself, is an interesting piece of potential data. As a comparison, when Rabbi Petachiah traveled from the German Empire to Central Asia and the Middle East in the 1170s, his travelogue begins with: "he set out from Prague, which is in Bohemia, going to Poland, from Poland to Kieff [Kyiv] in Russia [Rus], and from Russia [Rus] he went in six days to the river Dnieper."[243] This is the second sentence of the text and his journey only begins after his travels leave Rus, the extent of his, and his readers', known world. The Frankish embassy succeeded and brought back Anna Iaroslavna from Rus who came with many gifts and was subsequently married to King Henry.

One of the most high-profile marriages of a Rusian woman in medieval Europe was that of Evpraksia Vsevolodovna to Henry IV of the German Empire. This marriage has been discussed a great deal elsewhere, but it is worth mentioning three points of salient interest here.[244] The first is that the marriage was designed to create a relationship between Rus and the German Empire, largely to advance the cause of Henry IV's pope, Clement III. It is certainly possible that there were additional purposes for the marriage, especially from the Rusian side, but that Henry IV reached out to Rus for this purpose is relevant for the place of Rus in medieval Europe. He was perfectly willing, as was Clement III, to consider Rus as part of Christian Europe, inclusive of potential ties with the papacy. Second is the description of Evpraksia's arrival in the German Empire: she "arrived in this country with much pomp, with camels burdened with precious clothes and stones, and also with countless riches."[245] The imagery conjured by this description is

---

[242] Louis Paris, "Roger II, XLIVe eveque de Chalons, sa vieet sa mission en Russie," *La Chronique de Champagne* (1837), 94–96.

[243] Rabbi Petachia, *Travels of Rabbi Petachia of Ratisbon*, transl. Dr. A. Benisch (London: The Jewish Chronicle Office, 1856), 3.

[244] I have written about Evpraksia on several occasions, including "Evpraksia Vsevolodovna between East and West," *Russian History/Histoire Russe* 30:1–2 (2003), 23–34; "The Missing Rusian Women: The Case of Evpraksia Vsevolodovna," in *Putting together the Fragments: Writing Medieval Women's Lives*, ed. Amy Livingstone and Charlotte Newman Goldy (New York: Palgrave, 2012), 69–84.

[245] A. V. Nazarenko, *Drevniaia Rus' na mezhdunarodnykh putiakh: Mezhdistsiplinarnye ocherki kul'turnykh, torgovykh, politicheskikh sviazei IX-XII vekov* (Moskva: Iazyki Russkoi Kul'tury,

impressive as it calls to mind a caravan of animals each with panniers full of wealth, guided by a troupe of individuals all in place to serve the Rusian princess arriving for her marriage. The chronicler, typically, only notes the presence of Evpraksia herself, but a teenage girl is extraordinarily unlikely to have made the trip alone, and instead we see – between the lines – the presence of an entourage of Rusians who would now be resident in the German Empire. The similarity of this description with that of the arrival of the queen of Sheba (I Kings 10) only enhances the image of prosperity, wealth, and status of Evpraksia and her entourage, as it was no doubt intended to. Third, and finally, the Investiture Controversy precipitated a split between Henry IV and Evpraksia that saw her speaking at papal synods, including at Piacenza in 1095. The impact of a Rusian woman traveling and speaking, as the sources say she did, throughout Europe has been radically underestimated in the secondary literature. Additionally, relevant to Section 2 as well, this episode saw Pope Urban II send his newly written Feast for the Translation of the Relics of St. Nicholas to Rus. Pope Urban II wrote this feast in 1089 to celebrate the translation (read as "theft") of the relics from medieval Roman territory and their arrival in Bari. This feast was adopted by the Rusians, despite its deliberate antagonism toward the patriarchate of Constantinople; which put them in alignment not just with the papacy but with numerous of their neighbors who also saw a rise in the cult of St. Nicholas as this time as well.[246] Thus, though a brief recapitulation, Evpraksia's experience of two marriages in the German Empire and her return to Rus is emblematic of the kingdom of Rus as part of medieval Europe.

The connections between the ruling families of Europe via marriage made it possible to engage in a variety of interactions, especially with those other polities geographically closer to Rus. Involvement in conflicts is certainly one way to utilize the connections between families, as well as a rationale for making such connections. For instance, in the early twelfth century Iaroslav Sviatopolchich was engaged in an ongoing conflict with Volodimer Monomakh over a variety of issues. One could suggest that the two families had been struggling off and on since Monomakh's father participated in the usurpation of Iaroslav's grandfather back in the 1070s. This conflict came to a head in 1123 when Iaroslav summoned allies from the Árpád, Mieszkowice, and Přemyslid clans, along with other members of his own clan, to make a stand against

2001), 540 citing "Chronica ecclesiae Rosenfeldensis seu Hassefeldensis," in *Monumenta inedita rerum Germanicarum, precipue Bremensium*, ed. J. Vogt, vol. 1 (Bremen 1740), 125.

[246] Ildar H. Garipzanov, "Novgorod and the Veneration of Saints in Eleventh-Century Rus': A Comparative View," in *Saints and Their Lives on the Periphery: Veneration of Saints in Scandinavia and Eastern Europe (c. 1000–1200)*, ed. Haki Antonsson and Ildar H. Garipzanov. (Turnhout: Brepols, 2010), 139–142.

Monomakh.[247] The *Chronica de gestis Hungarorum* records that King Stephen II of Hungary led his soldiers himself, while Cosmas of Prague does not mention Rus but does note that Soběslav, who would become duke of Bohemia in 1125, was with Bolesław III and Stephen II in Poland in 1123.[248] Though Iaroslav was killed in the preparations for the battle, causing the alliance to dissolve, the prospect of soldiers and rulers from a wide swathe of central Europe gathering to participate in a conflict between members of the Volodimerovichi over rule in Rus is a fascinating one.

Ties with Poland had been close throughout this period for certain families among the Volodimerovichi of Rus. In the 1140s, Vsevolod Olgovich, the ruler in Kyiv, assisted his kinsman Władysław II multiple times. In 1142, Vsevolod sent his son Sviatoslav, along with two other Rusian rulers to assist Władysław in a conflict with Władysław's half-brother Bolesław.[249] The favor was returned in 1144 when Władysław brought troops to aid Vsevolod Olgovich in a conflict against Volodimerko of Galich. In this instance, Volodimerko also had allies, in the person of Ban Beloš of Hungary, the regent for the young Géza II.[250] This was a busy time, and in 1145, Vsevolod sent his brother Igor to Władysław to assist him and to help make peace among the Mieskowice. Peace was made, and for their assistance, the Rusians were given several towns, including the town of Wizna, which provided a better, more direct, Baltic connection.[251] Again in 1146, Vsevolod Olgovich called on assistance from Poland, and received it in the person of his son-in-law Bolesław the Tall; though, like the 1023 example, nothing came of this as Vsevolod died almost immediately.

Hungary too was particularly involved in Rusian conflicts, most often in the twelfth and thirteenth centuries, but the trend begins already in the early eleventh when Thietmar of Merseburg records that 500 Hungarian soldiers, along with 300 Germans and 1,000 Pechenegs, assisted Bolesław Chrobry in his attack on Kyiv on behalf of his son-in-law Sviatopolk.[252] Close marital ties in the second half of the twelfth century led to even closer relations in regard to conflict as well. Iziaslav Mstislavich, the ruler in Kyiv, called on Hungarian assistance already in 1148, but it was in 1149 when he was expelled by Iurii Dolgorukii that we see the Hungarian ruler's personal involvement for the first

247 Hypatian Chronicle, s.a. 1123.

248 Cosmas of Prague, Bk. 3, ch. 52; *The Illuminated Chronicle: Chronicle of the Deeds of the Hungarians from the Fourteenth-Century Illuminated Codex*, ed. and transl. János M. Bak and László Veszprémy (Budapest: Central European University Press, 2018), ch. 155, p. 287.

249 Hypatian Chronicle, s.a. 1142.

250 Hypatian Chronicle, s.a. 1144; Laurentian Chronicle, s.a. 1144.

251 A. B. Golovko. *Drevniaia Rus' i Pol'sha v politicheskikh vzaimo-otnosheniiakh X-pervoi treti XIII vv.* (Kiev: Nauka Dumka, 1988), 76–77.

252 *Ottonian Germany: The "Chronicon" of Thietmar of Merseburg*, transl. David A. Warner (Manchester: Manchester University Press, 2001), bk. 8, ch. 32.

time.[253] In that year, Iziaslav summoned a variety of aid from "his brother-in-law the king [Géza II], to his brother's son-in-law [generically "in-law"] Bolesław, and Mieszko, and Heinrich [Mieskowice from Poland], and his in-law Vladislav [II] ruler of the Czechs."[254] This was a major group, akin to what happened in 1123, and is a powerful statement about the ties a Rusian ruler could call upon amongst his neighbors. Though no battle resulted, the calling of his allies helped Iziaslav in his negotiations with Iurii Dolgorukii. They also laid the foundation for additional assistance quite quickly, as the next year Iziaslav sent his brother Volodimer to the Árpád court to again request assistance from Géza II.[255] These family ties were the warp and weft of relations between polities and they are on full display later this year when Iziaslav himself went to meet with his "in-law, the king and with his sister [Evfrosiniia], the queen . . . "[256] The meeting may have been a council of war, and in fact Géza warns Iziaslav that he would not be able to help much the next year as the "emperor of the Greeks" was planning a campaign against him, but it was one amongst family and that was highlighted by the terms used and the way the event proceeded. One of the first items on the agenda was the arrangement of a marriage between Iziaslav and Evfrosiniia's brother Volodimer to a daughter of Ban Beloš, Géza's former regent. As an interesting sidenote regarding the place of Rus in medieval Europe, this is the only known marital connection with the South Slavs during the eleventh and twelfth centuries. Though strong ties have been speculated, largely from the textual transmission record, there are almost no political or marital connections. These family relations continue in the 1150s, and in 1155, Volodimer sent his mother to the Hungarian court.[257] Though the chronicle entry expresses the situation almost entirely in regard to male relatives – "Then Volodimer Mstislavich sent his mother, Mstislav's wife, to the Hungarians, to his in-law the king. The king gave many possessions to his mother-in-law" – it seems quite likely that this woman, whose name we do not know, spent a good deal of her time with her daughter Queen Evfrosiniia. Though largely structured around conflict, this last example cements the familial relationships inherent in both medieval politics and in connecting Rus into medieval Europe. A, presumably, aging mother is sent to her daughter to be cared for; which, in this case, entails a trip from Rus to Hungary. The polity is not remarked upon, the journey is markedly uneventful, and instead we see the interconnectivity of the region on full display.

253 Hypatian Chronicle, s.a. 1148. 254 Hypatian Chronicle, s.a. 1149.

255 Hypatian Chronicle, s.a. 1150; *The Illuminated Chronicle*, ch. 168, p. 315.

256 Hypatian Chronicle, s.a. 1150. There is a break in the text at this point which is unfortunate as it would be quite interesting to find out what the chronicler said here.

257 Hypatian Chronicle, s.a. 1155.

While marital relationships underlay political connections, Rus and Rusians were also present in economic and other types of interactions around medieval Europe. Rusian trade ties were documented in writing already by the early tenth century as can be seen in the extant Raffelstettin regulations but are reinforced in sources from later in that century such as when Ibrahim ibn Yaqub traveled in central Europe in 965.[258] In Prague, which he labeled a trading city, he saw merchants from Rus and the Slavic lands coming from Cracow (which he notes is three weeks away), and Muslim and Jewish merchants from elsewhere. One of the clearest indications of trading connections with central Europe is the evidence of swords. Approximately 10% of the so-called Ulfbert swords, with a probable origin in the middle Rhine River region, have been found in Rus.[259] Though there are strong ties to Scandinavia in sword style and production, this model of Frankish sword came to be dominant in the tenth and eleventh centuries in Rus.[260] The eleventh and twelfth centuries also saw long range ties as Greenlandic ivory, still in situ in walrus skulls, was imported to the banks the Dnieper River for craftsmen to work with.[261] Also in the twelfth century, traders from Gotland and the German Empire both created their own trading entrepots in Novgorod.[262] Similarly, when Henry the Lion refounded Lübeck circa 1157, he invited the Rusians, among others on the Baltic, to trade there freely.[263]

The earliest Polish source, the *Deeds of the Princes of the Poles*, records at the beginning of Book One that Poland is "known to few apart from persons crossing to Rus for trade."[264] The place of Rus in Europe can be seen in the writings of Adam of Bremen who first places Rus in relationship to others in central Europe: "Across the Oder river the first people are the Pomeranians, next

[258] "Ibrāhīm ibn Ya'qūb on northern Europe 965," in *Ibn Fadlan and the Land of Darkness: Arab Travellers in the Far North*, transl. Paul Lunde and Caroline Stone (New York: Penguin, 2012), 162–168.

[259] A. N. Kirpichnikov, "Drevnerusskoe oruzhie: Vypusk pervyi, mechi I sabli IX-XIII vv," *Arkheologiia SSSR* E1-36 (1966), 38.

[260] For an excellent example of the Scandinavian style in Rus, see Ingmar Jansson, "Gotland Viewed from the Swedish Mainland," in *Viking-Age Trade: Silver, Slaves and Gotland*, ed. Jacek Gruszczyński, Marek Jankowiak and Jonathan Shepard (London and New York: Routledge, 2022), 338.

[261] James H. Barrett, Natalia Khamaiko, Giada Ferrari et al. "Walruses on the Dnieper: New Evidence for the Intercontinental Trade of Greenlandic Ivory in the Middle Ages," *Proceedings of the Royal Society B* (2022).

[262] Janet Martin, *Treasure of the Land of Darkness: The Fur Trade and its Significance for Medieval Russia* (Cambridge: Cambridge University Press, 1986), 49–50.

[263] *The Chronicle of the Slavs by Helmold, Priest of Bosau*, transl. Francis J. Tschan (New York: Columbia University Press, 1935), 229 ch. 86 (85).

[264] *Gesta Principum Polonorum: The Deeds of the Princes of the Poles*, transl. and ed. Paul W. Knoll and Frank Schaer (New York: Central European University Press, 2003), Bk. 1, pp. 10–11.

the Poles who are flanked here by the Prussians, there by the Bohemians, on the east by the Russians [Rusians]" and then notes travel distances to Rus in the Baltic: one month from Denmark, five days from Sweden.[265] Even Gilvase of Tilbury, writing in the Angevin world, knew of Rus and its location in regard to Scandinavia and Saxony, but also to England.[266] A trip between the two places by sea would be long, but easy, he suggests. And we see that during Henry II's reign there was at least one person from Rus in England. The pipe rolls for 1180-1181 record an Isaac of Rus in England at this time.[267] Jewish travelers, like Isaac, are commonly attested in the records. In 1171, a Benjamin of Vladimir (in Rus) is found in Köln, where he is falsely accused.[268] Around the same time, Rabbi Eleazer ben Isaac of Prague traveled to, and within, Rus and wrote about the Jewish communities he found there.[269]

Mercantile relations are documented between Rus and the rest of medieval Europe in both archaeological and textual sources. The east-west trade route which ran from the German Empire (particularly Regensburg and Mainz) through Prague, Cracow, and Przemysl to Kyiv is seen in both kinds of sources, some of which have already been noted. Dirhams, which are comparatively rare in central Europe, are found in tenth-century deposits around Mainz.[270] The assumption has been that they arrived there from Rus, which was a major source of dirhams to the northern world at this time as well.[271] But even after the end of the proliferation of dirhams in the tenth century, the east-west engagement persisted. Attesting to this is the find of numerous denarii in the small towns of northern Rus which implemented the fur harvesting trade.[272] The presence of central European coinage not just in Rus, but in rural Rus, suggests the level of

[265] Adam of Bremen, *The History of the Archbishops of Hamburg-Bremen*, Francis J. Tschan, transl. (New York: Columbia University Press, 2002), Bk. 2, ch. 21 (18), schol. 14 (15); Bk. 4, ch. 11 and schol. 126.

[266] Gervase of Tilbury, "Gervasii Tilleberiensis Otiis Imperialibus," *Monumenta Germaniae Historica Scriptores* 27, ed. F. Liebermann and R. Pauli (Leipzig: Karl W. Hiersemann, 1925), 371.

[267] *The Great Roll of the Pipe for the Twenty-Seventh Year of the Reign of King Henry the Second, A.D. 1180–1181*, 134.

[268] *Hebräische Berichte über die Judenverfolgungen während der Kreuzzüge*, ed. and transl. A. Neubauer and M. Stern. (Berlin, 1896), 206.

[269] J. Brutzkus, "Trade with Eastern Europe, 800–1200," *The Economic History Review* 13:1/2 (1943), 36.

[270] Brutzkus, "Trade with Eastern Europe," 33.

[271] For dirhams in the north, see the recent: Marek Jankowiak, "Dirham Flows into Northern and Eastern Europe and the Rhythms of the Slave Trade with the Islamic World," in *Viking-Age Trade: Silver, Slaves and Gotland*, ed. Jacek Gruszczyński, Marek Jankowiak and Jonathan Shepard (London and New York: Routledge, 2022), 105–131.

[272] N. A. Makarov, "The Fur Trade in the Economy of the Northern Borderlands of Medieval Russia," in *The Archaeology of Medieval Novgorod in Context: Studies in Centre-Periphery Relations*, ed. Mark A. Brisbane, Nikolaj A. Makarov, and Evgenij N. Nosov (Oxford: Oxbow Books, 2012), 387.

interpenetration of the economies across medieval Europe, inclusive of Rus. Rusian merchants appear in numerous law codes and royal acts well into the twelfth and thirteenth centuries. In 1191, Ottakar IV of Styria reiterated the fees for traders which his father had created: "Carts going to or coming from Ruzia shall pay 16 pence (denarios)."[273] The next year, Leopold V of Austria fixed the fees for traders going to and from Rus, and after the combination of Austria and Styria, Leopold and his son Frederick reiterated these measures and laid out the incoming and outgoing trade goods. Next door, the Hungarian king Imre, in 1198, mentioned the continuing presence of Rusian merchants in his kingdom bringing furs and horses.[274] These traders were well established in central Europe, after the point at which some have conjectured a break between the Latin and Orthodox worlds. In fact, Rusians, and potentially traders, were even noted at the highest levels of political conversation, as three letters included by Otto of Freising suggest.[275] The first is a letter from Emperor Conrad to Emperor John II Komnenos in which he refers to a matter concerning a group of Rusians who had taken money from envoys of the Germans. There are no specifics recorded in the letter, nor a rationale for why it is under discussion between these two rulers. Some have suggested that its presence here indicates that the Germans viewed Rus as part of the Roman Empire, though this reading seems to be based on modern ideas.[276] John's letter is preserved, in which he acknowledges the matter and suggests that he has done what he could. Finally, Conrad writes to John's son and successor Manuel referencing the matter once more. None of these letters specify anything, but for our purposes they do not need to, as they are simply indicative of Rus as part of the interactions of the two major emperors in medieval Europe.

The material provided here is truly only the tip of the iceberg in terms of the placement of Rus in the midst of medieval Europe. A trawl through the Monumenta Germaniae Historica will show dozens of mentions of Rus and Rusians. The Scandinavian sources discuss the presence of Rusian traders and envoys in *Heimskringla, Morkinskinna, Fagrskinna*, and many more in both Old Norse and Latin. Sources from England, France, Hungary, and Poland include mentions of Rus, and, as is well known, the papacy corresponds with Rusian rulers in the eleventh, twelfth, and thirteenth centuries. Oddly for our common perception of Rus, the place where we find the fewest mentions is in

273 Brutzkus, "Trade with Eastern Europe," 35.

274 *Codex Diplomaticus Hungariae ecclesiasticus ac civilis*, vol. 7 (5), ed. Georgius Fejér (Buda: 1841), 143.

275 Otto of Freising, Bk. 1, ch. 25.

276 V. Vasil'evskii, "Drevniaia torgovlia Kieva s Regensburgom," *Zhurnal ministerstva narodnogo prosveshcheniia* (1888): 139–140.

Greek sources. Rus is present in the tenth-century material, but in the vast eleventh- and twelfth-century source base written by such famous names as Michael Psellos, Michael Attaliates, and Anna Komnena Rus rarely, if ever appears. This is not to minimize the medieval Roman Empire or their contributions to Rus or medieval Europe in any way. Rather, it is essential to approach the medieval world on its own terms and via the extant testaments first, and only then develop ideas about what did or did not happen. Setting aside modern preconceptions and looking at the material listed here it is quite easy to see that the place of the kingdom of Rus was **in** medieval Europe.

Bibliography

Primary Sources

"The 971 Treaty." Transl. Daniel Kaiser. In *The Laws of Rus' – Tenth to Fifteenth Centuries*. Transl. And ed. Daniel H. Kaiser. Salt Lake City, Utah: Charles Schlacks Jr., 1992: 13.

Adam of Bremen. *The History of the Archbishops of Hamburg-Bremen*. Transl. Francis J. Tschan. New York: Columbia University Press, 2002.

"Addition Decima: Leges Portorii c.a. 906." In *Monumenta Germaniae Historica. Leges* tom III. Hannover: Impensis Bibliopolii Avlici Hahniani, 1863: 480–481.

Aktovye pechati drevnei rusi X-XV vv. Vol 1. Pechati X-nachala XIII v. Ed. V. L. Ianin. Moscow: Nauka, 1970.

"Annalista Saxo." In *Monumenta Germaniae Historica: Scriptores* 6. Hannover: Impensis Bibliopolii Avlici Hahniani, 1844: 542–777.

The Annals of St-Bertin. Transl. Janet L. Nelson. New York: Manchester University Press, 1991.

The Chronicle of Novgorod, 1016–1471. Ed. and transl. Robert Michel and Nevill Forbes. Royal Historical Society, 1914.

The Chronicle of the Slavs by Helmold, Priest of Bosau. Transl. Francis J. Tschan. New York: Columbia University Press, 1935.

Clarius. *Chronique de Sant-Pierre-le-vif de sens, diter de Clarius*. Ed. Robert-Henri Bautier and Monique Gilles. Paris: Centre national de la recherche scientifique, 1979.

Codex Diplomaticus Hungariae ecclesiasticus ac civilis. vol. 7 (5). Ed. Georgius Fejér. Buda: 1841.

Constantine Porphyrogennetos: The Book of Ceremonies. Transl. Ann Moffatt and Maxeme Tall. Leiden: Brill, 2012.

Cosmas of Prague. *The Chronicle of the Czechs by Cosmas of Prague*. Transl. Lisa Wolverton. Washington, DC: The Catholic University of America Press, 2009.

"The First Treaty of Novgorod with Tver' Grand Prince Iaroslav Iaroslavich [1230–71], ca. 1264–65." Transl. Daniel Kaise. In *The Laws of Rus' – Tenth to Fifteenth Centuries*, transl. and ed. Daniel H. Kaiser. Salt Lake City, Utah: Charles Schlacks Jr., 1992: 67–68.

Fletcher, Giles. "Of the Russe Commonwealth: Or, Maner of Governement by the Russe emperour (Commonly Called the Emperour of Moskovia) with the Manners and Fashions of the People of that Countrey." In *Russia at the Close of the Sixteenth Century*. Ed. Edward A. Bond. London: Hakluyt Society, 1856: 1–152.

Gervase of Tilbury. "Gervasii Tilleberiensis Otiis Imperialibus." In *Monumenta Germaniae Historica Scriptores* 27. Ed. F. Liebermann and R. Pauli. Leipzig: Karl W. Hiersemann, 1925: 359–394.

Gesta Principum Polonorum: The Deeds of the Princes of the Poles. Transl. and ed. Paul W. Knoll and Frank Schaer. New York: Central European University Press, 2003.

The Great Roll of the Pipe for the Twenty-Seventh Year of the Reign of King Henry the Second, A.D. 1180–1181. London: St. Catherine Press, 1914.

Hebräische Berichte über die Judenverfolgungen während der Kreuzzüge. Ed. and transl. A. Neubauer and M. Stern. Berlin: L. Simion, 1896.

Heinrich, Lisa. "The Kievan Chronicle: A Translation and Commentary." PhD Dissertation, Vanderbilt University, 1977.

Henricus Lettus. *Heinrici Chronicion Lyvoniae*. Ed. Wilhelm Arndt. Hannover: Impensis Bibliopolii Hahniani, 1874.

Henricus Lettus. *The Chronicle of Henry of Livonia*. Transl. James A. Brundage. New York: Columbia University Press, 2003.

Histoire de Yahya-ibn-Sa'īd d'Antioche. Transl. I. Kratchkovsky and A. Vasiliev. *Patrologia Orientalis* 18 (1924) and 23 (1932).

"Ibn Khurradādhbih on the routes of the Rādhānīya and the Rūs c. 830." In *Ibn Fadlan and the Land of Darkness: Arab Travellers in the Far North*. Transl. Paul Lunde and Caroline Stone. New York: Penguin, 2012: 111–112.

"Ibrāhīm ibn Ya'qūb on northern Europe 965." In *Ibn Fadlan and the Land of Darkness: Arab Travellers in the Far North*. Transl. Paul Lunde and Caroline Stone. New York: Penguin, 2012: 162–168.

Ilarion. "Sermon on Law and Grace." In *Sermons and Rhetoric of Kievan Rus'*. Transl. Simon Franklin. Cambridge, MA: Harvard University Press, 1991: 3–30.

The Illuminated Chronicle: Chronicle of the Deeds of the Hungarians from the Fourteenth-Century Illuminated Codex. Ed. and transl. János M. Bak and László Veszprémy. Budapest: Central European University Press, 2018.

"Istakhrī on the Khazars and their neighbours, c. 951." In *Ibn Fadlan and the Land of Darkness: Arab Travellers in the Far North*. Transl. Paul Lunde and Caroline Stone. New York: Penguin, 2012: 153–159.

John Skylitzes. *A Synopsis of Byzantine History, 811–1057*. Transl. John Wortley. Cambridge: Cambridge University Press, 2010.

"Khozhenie Daniila, igumena Russkoi zemli." In *Kniga khozhenii: Zapiski russkikh puteshestvennikov XI-XV vv.* Moscow: Sovetskaia Rossiia, 1984: 27–79.

"Lamberti annalium para prior ab O.C. – 1039." In *Monumenta Germaniae Historica: Scriptores* 3. Hannover: Impensis Bibliopolii Avlici Hahniani, 1839: 22–29, 33–69, 90–102.

Lampert of Hersfeld. *The Annals of Lampert of Hersfeld*. Transl. I. S. Robinson. Manchester: Manchester University Press, 2015.

Leo the Deacon. *The History of Leo the Deacon: Byzantine Military Expansion in the Tenth Century*. Transl. Alice-Mary Talbot and Denis F. Sullivan. Washington, DC: Dumbarton Oaks Research Library and Collection, 2005.

Loseva, O. V. *Russkie Mesiateslovy XI–XIV vekov*. Moscow: Pamiatniki istoricheskoi mysli, 2001.

Mango, Cyril. *The Homilies of Photius Patriarch of Constantinople*. Cambridge, MA: Harvard University Press, 1958.

"Mas'ūdī on a Viking Raid on the Casptian, c. 913." In *Ibn Fadlan and the Land of Darkness: Arab Travellers in the Far North*. Transl. Paul Lunde and Caroline Stone. New York: Penguin, 2012: 144–146.

Medieval Russian Laws. Transl. George Vernadsky. New York: Oxford University Press, 1947.

"Mercandi Causa." In *Monumenta Germaniae Historica: Capitularia regum Francorum*, vol. 2, Ed. Victor Krause. Hanover: Impensis Bibliopolii, 1897.

Michael Psellos. *Fourteen Byzantine Rulers: The Chronographia of Michael Psellus*. Transl. E. R. A. Sewter. New York: Penguin, 1966.

Novgorodskaia pervaia letopis' starshego i mladshego izvodov, vol. 3, Polnoe sobranie russkikh letopisei. Moscow: Iazyki slavianskoi kultury, 2000.

The Old Rus' Kievan and Galician-Volhynian Chronicles: The Ostroz'kyj (Xlebnikov) and četvertyns'kyj (Pogodin) codices. Omeljan Pritsak, Introduction. Cambridge, MA: Harvard University Press, 1990.

Otto of Freising. *Gesta Friderici Imperatoris*. Accessed online at The Latin Library.

Ottonian Germany: The "Chronicon" of Thietmar of Merseburg. Transl. David A. Warner. Manchester: Manchester University Press, 2001.

The Paterik of the Kievan Caves Monastery. Transl. Muriel Heppell. Cambridge, MA: Harvard Ukrainian Research Institute, 1989.

Photii patriarchae Constantinopolitani epistulae et amphilochia. Ed. Vasileios Laourdas, and Leendert Gerrit Westerink. Leipzig: BSB B. G. Teubner Verlagsgesellschaft, 1983.

Polnoe sobranie russkikh letopisei: Tom IX. Letopisnyi sbornik, imenuemyi: Patriarshei ili Nikonovskoi letopis'iu. Moscow: Iazyki russkoi kul'tury, 2000.

The Povest' vremennykh let: An Interlinear Collation and Paradosis. Compiled and edited by Donald Ostrowski, with David Birnbaum and Horace G. Lunt. Cambridge, MA: Harvard University Press, 2004.

Rabbi Petachia. *Travels of Rabbi Petachia of Ratisbon*. Transl. Dr. A. Benisch. London: The Jewish Chronicle Office, 1856.

Reginonis Abbatis Prumiensis Chronicon cum continuation Treverensi. Ed. Frederick Kurze. Hannover: Impensis Biblipolii Hahniani, 1890.

The Register of Pope Gregory VII, 1073–1085. Ed. and transl. H. E. J. Cowdrey. Oxford: Oxford University Press, 2002.

The Russian Primary Chronicle: Laurentian Text. Transl. and ed. Samuel Hazzard Cross and Olgerd P. Sherbowitz-Wetzor. Cambridge, MA: The Mediaeval Academy of America, 1953.

"The Russkaia Pravda: The Short Redaction (Academy Copy)." Transl. Daniel Kaiser. In *The Laws of Rus' – Tenth to Fifteenth Centuries*. Transl. and Ed. Daniel H. Kaiser. Salt Lake City, Utah: Charles Schlacks Jr., 1992: 15–19.

"The Russkaia Pravda: The Expanded Redaction (Trinity Copy)." Transl. Daniel Kaiser. In *The Laws of Rus' – Tenth to Fifteenth Centuries*. Transl. and ed. Daniel H. Kaiser. Salt Lake City, Utah: Charles Schlacks Jr., 1992: 20–34.

"Statute of the Novgorod Prince Vsevolod [1135–37] on Church Courts, [Church] People, and Trade Measures." Transl. Daniel Kaiser. In *The Laws of Rus' – Tenth to Fifteenth Centuries*. Transl. and ed. Daniel H. Kaiser. Salt Lake City, Utah: Charles Schlacks Jr., 1992: 59–63.

Theophanes Continuatus. *Chronographiae quae Theophanis Continuati nomine fertur Libri I-IV*. Ed. Jeffrey Michael Featherstone and Juan Signes-Codoñer. Berlin: De Gruyter, 2015.

"Treaty of Novgorod with Tver' Grand Prince Mikhail Iaroslavich [1271–1318], 1304–5." Transl. Daniel Kaiser. In *The Laws of Rus' – Tenth to Fifteenth Centuries*. Transl. and ed. Daniel H. Kaiser. Salt Lake City, Utah: Charles Schlacks Jr., 1992: 69–71.

Vysotskii, S. A. *Kievskie graffiti XI-XVII vv*. Kiev: Naukova Dumka, 1985.

"Wilhelmi Abbatis Genealogia Regum Danorum." In *Scriptores minores historiae danicae medii ævi*, vol. 1 of 2. Ed. M. C. L. Getz. Copenhagen: I Kommission hos G. E. C. Gad, 1917: 145–194.

Secondary Sources

Amiranashvili, Sh. J. *Georgian Art*. Tbilisi: Tbilisi University Press, 1968.

Arnold, John. "Believing in Belief: Gibbon, Latour and the Social History of Religion." *Past & Present* 260 (2023): 236–268.

Barrett, James H., Natalia Khamaiko, Giada Ferrari et al. "Walruses on the Dnieper: New Evidence for the Intercontinental Trade of Greenlandic Ivory in the Middle Ages." *Proceedings of the Royal Society B* (2022).

Bedos-Rezak, Brigitte. “Medieval Women in French Sigillographic Sources.” In *Medieval Women and the Sources of Medieval History.* Ed. Joel T. Rosenthal. Athens and London: University of Georgia Press, 1990: 1–36.

Brutzkus, J. “Trade with Eastern Europe, 800–1200.” *The Economic History Review* 13:1/2 (1943): 31–41.

Bury, J. B. “Introduction.” In *The Cambridge Medieval History.* Vol. IV *The Eastern Roman Empire (717–1453).* New York: The MacMillan, 1923: vii–xiv.

Butler, Francis. *Enlightener of Rus': The Image of Vladimir Sviatoslavich across the Centuries.* Bloomington: Slavica, 2002.

Butler, Francis. “Wenceslas: The Saint and his name in Kievan Rus.” *Slavic and East European Journal* 48:1 (2004): 63–78.

Byrnes, Robert F. *V. O. Kliuchevskii, Historian of Russia.* Bloomington: Indiana University Press, 1995.

van Caenegem, R. “Government, Law and Society.” In *The Cambridge History of Medieval Political thought, c. 350–1450.* Ed. J. H. Burns. Cambridge: Cambridge University Press, 1988: 174–210.

Carlsson, Dan. “Gotland: Silver Island.” In *Viking-Age Trade: Silver, Slaves and Gotland.* Ed. Jacek Gruszczyński, Marek Jankowiak and Jonathan Shepard. London and New York: Routledge, 2022: 225–241.

Cook, William R. and Ronald B. Herzman. *The Medieval World View: An Introduction.* New York and Oxford: Oxford University Press [3rd ed.], 2012.

Cowdrey, H. E. J. *Pope Gregory VII 1073–1085.* Oxford: Clarendon Press, 1998.

Curta, Florin. *Eastern Europe in the Middle Ages (500–1300).* Leiden and Boston: Brill, 2019.

Cutler, Anthony. “Garda, Källunge and the Byzantine Tradition on Gotland.” *Art Bulletin* 51:3 (1969): 257–266.

Danylenko, Andriy and Christian Raffensperger. “Rus and the South.” In *Encyclopedia of Slavic Languages and Linguistics.* Ed. Marc L. Greenberg. Leiden: Brill, 2024 [forthcoming].

Drobyshcheva, M. M. “Graffito No. 25 iz Sofii Kievskoi: Chto my znaem o pokupke ‘Boianovoi zemli’?” *Vestnik Permskogo Universiteta* 1:48 (2020): 130–145.

Dvornik, Francis. *Byzantine Missions among the Slavs.* New Brunswick: Rutgers University Press, 1970.

Ericsson. K. “The Earliest Conversion of the Rus' to Christianity.” *Slavonic and East European Review* 44:102 (1966): 98–121.

Fowden, Garth. *Empire to Commonwealth: Consequences of Monotheism in Late Antiquity.* Princeton: Princeton University Press, 1993.

Franklin, Simon and Jonathan Shepard. *The Emergence of Rus, 750–1200.* New York: Longman, 1996.

Franklin, Simon. *Writing, Society and Culture in Early Rus', c. 950–1300.* Cambridge: Cambridge University Press, 2002.

Garipzanov, Ildar. "The Annals of St. Bertin (839) and *Chacanus* of the *Rhos*." *Ruthenica* 5:1 (2006): 7–11.

Garipzanov, Ildar H. "Novgorod and the Veneration of Saints in Eleventh-Century Rus': A Comparative View." In *Saints and Their Lives on the Periphery: Veneration of Saints in Scandinavia and Eastern Europe (c. 1000–1200).* Ed. Haki Antonsson and Ildar H. Garipzanov. Turnhout: Brepols, 2010: 115–146.

Golovko, A. B. *Drevniaia Rus' i Pol'sha v politicheskikh vzaimo-otnosheniiakh X-pervoi treti XIII vv.* Kiev: Nauka Dumka, 1988.

Gordin, A. M. "Zametki o palomnicheskikh graffiti abbatstva sen-zhil'." In *V kamne i v bronze: Sbornik statei v chest' Anny Peskovoi*. Ed. A. E. Musin and O. A. Shcheglova. St. Petersburg: RAN, 2017: 95–103.

Granberg, Jonas. *Veche in the Chronicles of Medieval Rus: A Study of Functions and Terminology.* Göteborg: Göteborg University, 2004.

Hollister, C. Warren. "Normandy, France and the Anglo-Norman Regnum." *Speculum* 51:2 (1976): 202–242.

Hughes, Lindsay. "Russia." In *A Companion to Eighteenth-Century Europe*. Ed. Peter H. Wilson. New York: Blackwell, 2008: 225–243.

Hupalo, V. "Khristianskie relikvii palomnikov iz kniazheskogo zvenigoroda." In *V kamne i v bronze: Sbornik statei v chest' Anny Peskovoi*. Ed. A. E. Musin and O. A. Shcheglova. St. Petersburg: RAN, 2017: 117–123.

Ianin, V. L. *Novgorodskie posadniki*. Moscow: Izdatel'stvo Moskovskogo universiteta, 1962.

Ianin, V. L. "Russkaia kniaginia Olisava-Gertruda i ee syn Iaropolk." *Numizmatika i epigrafika* 4 (1963): 142–164.

Jackson, Tatjana N. "The Cult of St Olaf and Early Novgorod." In *Saints and Their Lives on the Periphery: Veneration of Saints in Scandinavia and Eastern Europe (c. 1000–1200)*. Ed. Haki Antonsson and Ildar H. Garipzanov. Turnhout: Brepols, 2010: 147–170.

Jankowiak, Marek. "Dirham Flows into Northern and Eastern Europe and the Rhythms of the Slave Trade with the Islamic World." In *Viking-Age Trade: Silver, Slaves and Gotland*. Ed. Jacek Gruszczyński, Marek Jankowiak and Jonathan Shepard. London and New York: Routledge, 2022: 105–131.

Jansson, Ingmar. "Gotland Viewed from the Swedish Mainland." In *Viking-Age Trade: Silver, Slaves and Gotland*. Ed. Jacek Gruszczyński, Marek Jankowiak and Jonathan Shepard. London and New York: Routledge, 2022: 315–357.

Kaldellis, Anthony. *Romanland: Ethnicity and Empire in Byzantium*. Cambridge, MA: Harvard University Press, 2019.

Khrustalev, D. G. *Razyskaniia o Efreme Pereiaslavskom*. Saint Petersburg: Evraziia, 2002.

Kirpichnikov, A. N. "Drevnerusskoe oruzhie: Vypusk pervyi, mechi I sabli IX-XIII vv." *Arkheologiia SSSR* E1-36 (1966): 5–181.

Kivelson, Valerie A. and Ronald Grigor Suny. *Russia's Empires*. Oxford: Oxford University Press, 2017.

Kliuchevsky, V. O. *A History of Russia*. Vol. 1. Transl. C. J. Hogarth. New York: Russell and Russell, 1960.

Lewis, Andrew W. *Royal Succession in Capetian France: Studies on Familial Order and the State*. Cambridge, MA: Cambridge University Press, 1981.

Livingstone, Amy. *Out of Love for My Kin: Aristocratic Family Life in the Lands of the Loire, 1000–1200*. Cornell: Cornell University Press, 2010.

Lomonosov, M. *Drevniaia Rossiiskaia istoriia ot nachala rossiiskogo naroda do konchiny velikogo kniazia Iaroslava Pervogo ili do 1054 goda*. St. Petersburg: pri Imperatorskoĭ Akademii nauk, 1766.

Makarov, N. "Traders in the Forest: The Northern Periphery of Rus' in the Medieval Trade Network." In *Pre-Modern Russia and its World: Essays in Honor of Thomas S. Noonan*. Ed. Kathryn L. Reyerson, Theofanis G. Stavrou, James D. Tracy. Wiesbaden: Harrassowitz, 2006: 115–133.

Makarov, N. A. "The Fur Trade in the Economy of the Northern Borderlands of Medieval Russia." In *The Archaeology of Medieval Novgorod in Context: Studies in Centre-Periphery Relations*. Ed. Mark A. Brisbane, Nikolaj A. Makarov, and Evgenij N. Nosov. Oxford: Oxbow Books, 2012: 381–390.

Martin, Janet. *Treasure of the Land of Darkness: The Fur Trade and its Significance for Medieval Russia*. Cambridge: Cambridge University Press, 1986.

Martin, Therese. "Exceptions and Assumptions: Women in Medieval Art History." In *Reassessing the Roles of Women as "Makers" of Medieval Art and Architecture*. Ed. Therese Martin. Leiden and Boston: Brill, 2012: 1–36.

Nazarenko, A. V. *Drevniaia Rus' na mezhdunarodnykh putiakh: Mezhdistsiplinarnye ocherki kul'turnykh, torgovykh, politicheskikh sviazei IX-XII vekov*. Moscow: Iazyki Russkoi Kul'tury, 2001.

Nazarenko, A.V. "Mitropolii iaroslavichei vo vtoroi polovine XI veka." In *Drevniaia Rus' i Slaviane*. Moscow: RAN, 2009: 207–245.

Nazarenko, Tatiana. "East Slavic Visual Writing: The Inception of Tradition." *Canadian Slavonic Papers / Revue Canadienne des Slavistes* 43:2–3 (2001): 209–225.

Nelson, Robert S. *The Iconography of Preface and Miniature in the Byzantine Gospel Book*. New York: New York University Press for the College Art Association, 1980.

Noonan, Thomas S. "Scandinavians in European Russia." In *The Oxford Illustrated History of the Vikings*. Ed. Peter Sawyer. Oxford: Oxford University Press, 1997:134–155.

Noonan, Thomas S. "Why the Vikings First Came to Russia." In *The Islamic World, Russia and the Vikings, 750–900: The Numismatic Evidence*. Brookfield, Vt.: Ashgate, 1998: 321–348.

Obolensky, Dimitri. *The Byzantine Commonwealth, Eastern Europe 500–1453*. London: Weidenfeld and Nicolson, 1971.

Ostrowski, Donald. "The Account of Volodimer's Conversion in the *Povest' vremennykh let*: A Chiasmus of Stories." *Harvard Ukrainian Studies* 28:1–4 (2006[actually 2010]): 567–580.

Paris, Louis. "Roger II, XLIVe eveque de Chalons, sa vieet sa mission en Russie." *La Chronique de Champagne* 2 (1837): 89–99.

Pekarska, Ljudmila. *Jewellery of Princely Kiev: The Kiev Hoards in the British Museum and the Metropolitan Museum of Art and Related Material*. Ed. Barry Ager and Dafydd Kidd. Mainz and London: Verlag des Römisch-Germanischen Zentralmuseums, 2011.

Pevny, Olenka Z. "Kievan Rus'." In *The Glory of Byzantium: Art and Culture of the Middle Byzantine Era, A.D. 843–1261*. Ed. Helen C. Evans and William D. Wixom. New York: Metropolitan Museum of Art, 1997: 280–319.

Plokhy, Serhii. *Unmaking Imperial Russia: Mykhailo Hrushevsky and the Writing of Ukrainian History*. Toronto: University of Toronto Press, 2005.

Poppe, A. V. "Russkie mitropolii konstantinopol'skoi patriarkhii v XI stoletii." *Vizantiiskii Vremennik* 28 (1968): 98–104.

Poppe, Andrzej. "Leontios, Abbot of Patmos, Candidate for the Metropolitan See of Rus'." In *Christian Russia in the Making*. Aldershot and Burlington: Ashgate Variorum, 2007: 1–13.

Popova, O. S. "Ostromirovo evangelie. Miniatiury i ornament." In *Ostromirovo evangelie i sovremennye issledovaniia. Rukopisnoi traditsii. Novozavetnykh tekstov*. Ed. S. A. Daydova. Saint Petersburg: Rossiiskaia natsional'naia biblioteka, 2010: 60–84.

Raffensperger, Christian. "Evpraksia Vsevolodovna between East and West." *Russian History/Histoire Russe* 30:1–2 (2003): 23–34.

Raffensperger, Christian. *Reimagining Europe: Kievan Rus' in the Medieval World*. Cambridge, MA: Harvard University Press, 2012.

Raffensperger, Christian. "The Missing Rusian Women: The Case of Evpraksia Vsevolodovna." In *Putting together the Fragments: Writing Medieval Women's Lives*. Ed. Amy Livingstone and Charlotte Newman Goldy. New York: Palgrave, 2012: 69–84.

Raffensperger, Christian. *Ties of Kinship: Genealogy and Dynastic Marriage in Kyivan Rus'*. Cambridge, MA: Harvard Ukrainian Research Institute, 2016.

Raffensperger, Christian. *The Kingdom of Rus*. Leeds: Arc Humanities Press, 2017.

Raffensperger, Christian. "Kyivan Rus: A Complicated Kingdom." In *How Medieval Europe was Ruled*. Ed. Christian Raffensperger. New York: Routledge, 2023: 176–190.

Raffensperger, Christian. *Rulers and Rulership in the Arc of Medieval Europe*. New York: Routledge, 2023.

Raffensperger, Christian. *Name Unknown: The Life of a Rusian Queen*. New York: Routledge, 2024.

Raffensperger, Christian and Donald Ostrowski. *The Ruling Families of Rus: Clan, Family, and Kingdom*. London: Reaktion Books, 2023.

Riasanovsky, Nicholas V. *A History of Russia*. 5th ed. New York, Oxford: Oxford University Press, 1993.

Rosenwein, Barbara H. *A Short History of the Middle Ages*. Toronto: University of Toronto Press, 2009 [3rd ed.].

Schaeken, Jos. "Comments on Birchbark Documents Found in the Twenty-First Century: Zamechaniia k berestniam gramotam, naidennym v XXI veke." *Russian Linguistics* 41 (2017): 123–149.

Selart, Anti. *Livonia, Rus' and the Baltic Crusades in the Thirteenth Century*. Transl. Fiona Robb. Leiden and Boston: Brill, 2015.

Shchaveleva, N. I. "Kniaz' Iaropolk Iziaslavich i khristianskaia tserkov' XI v." In *Vostochnaia evropa v drevnosti I srednevekov'e: X Cheteniia k 80-letiiu chlena-korrespondenta AN SSSR Vladimira Terent'evicha Pashuto*. Ed. E. A. Mel'nikova. Moscow: RAN, 1998: 132–136.

Shepard, Jonathan. "Why Did the Russians Attack Byzantium in 1043?" *Byzantinisch-Neugriechische Jahrbücher* 22. Ed. Nikos A. Bees. Athens: Verlag de BNJ, 1985: 147–212.

Shepard, Jonathan. "Rus'." In *Christianization and the Rise of Christian Monarchy: Scandinavia, Central Europe and Rus', c. 900–1200*. Ed. Nora Berend. Cambridge: Cambridge University Press, 2007: 369–416.

Shorter Oxford English Dictionary. Vol. 1: A-M. Oxford: Oxford University Press, 2007 [6th ed.].

Slovar' russkogo iazyka, X-XVII vv. Vol. 4 (G-D). Moscow: Nauka, 1977.

Soldat, Cornelia. *Erschreckende Geschichten in der Darstellung von Moskovitern und Osmanen in den deutschen Flugschriften des 16. und 17. Jahrhunderts / Stories of Atrocities in Sixteenth and Seventeenth Century German Pamphlets about the Russians and Turks*. Lewiston – Queenston – Lampeter: Edwin Mellen Press, 2014.

Stefanovich, P. S. *Boiare, otroki, druzhiny: Voenno-politicheskaia elita Rusi v X-XI vekakh*. Moscow: Indrik, 2012.

Vasil'evskii, V. "Drevniaia torgovlia Kieva s Regensburgom." *Zhurnal ministerstva narodnogo prosveshcheniia* (1888), Vol. 258: 121–150.

Vernadsky, George. *Kievan Russia*. New Haven: Yale University Press, 1948.

Vilkul, Tatiana. "People and Boyars in the Old Russian Chronicles of the 11th–13th Centuries: Narrative Modelling of Social Identities." In *Imagined Communities: Constructing Collective Identities in Medieval Europe*. Ed. Andrzej Pleszczyński, Joanna Sobiesiak, Michał Tomaszek, Przemysław Tyszka. Leiden and Boston: Brill, 2018: 179–203.

Wheeler, Marcus. *The Oxford Russian-English Dictionary*. 2nd ed. Oxford: Oxford University Press, 1992.

White, Monica. *Military Saints in Byzantium and Rus, 900–1200*. Cambridge: Cambridge University Press, 2013.

Wolff, Larry. *Inventing Eastern Europe: The Map of Civilization on the Mind of the Enlightenment*. Stanford: Stanford University Press, 1994.

Zajac, Natalia Anna Makaryk. "Women between West and East: The Inter-Rite Marriages of the Kyivan Rus' Dynasty, ca. 1000–1204." PhD Dissertation; University of Toronto, 2017.

Zakharii, R. "The Historiography of Normanist and Anti-Normanist Theories on the Origin of Rus': A Review of Modern Historiography and Major Sources on Varangian Controversy and Other Scandinavian Concepts of the Origins of Rus'." University of Oslo: Centre for Viking and Medieval Studies, The Faculty of Arts, 2002.

Cambridge Elements

Rethinking Byzantium

Leonora Neville

University of Wisconsin Madison

Leonora Neville is the John and Jeanne Rowe Professor of Byzantine History and Vilas Distinguished Achievement Professor at the University of Wisconsin-Madison. She has written extensively on eastern Roman society, particularly on authority in provincial communities, history writing, gender, and the importance of the classical past for medieval Roman culture.

Darlene Brooks Hedstrom

Brandeis University

Darlene Brooks Hedstrom is the Myra and Robert Kraft and Jacob Hiatt Chair in Christian Studies at Brandeis University. She is an archaeologist and historian of the late antique Mediterranean world. Her works examine the intersection of objects, religious practice, monasticism, and the history of archaeology.

About the Series

Elements in Rethinking Byzantium offer crisp and accessible introductions to vibrant current research on medieval eastern Roman society and culture which sets them within broader schemas of pre-modern history and cultural study. Individual Elements address various aspects of visual and literary cultures, history, and religion in the territory and cultural sphere of the Roman Empire, broadly conceived, from the fourth to fifteenth centuries CE.

Cambridge Elements

Rethinking Byzantium

Elements in the Series

Kyivan Rus in Medieval Europe
Christian Raffensperger

A full series listing is available at: www.cambridge.org/RTHB

For EU product safety concerns, contact us at Calle de José Abascal, 56–1°, 28003 Madrid, Spain or eugpsr@cambridge.org.

www.ingramcontent.com/pod-product-compliance
Ingram Content Group UK Ltd.
Pitfield, Milton Keynes, MK11 3LW, UK
UKHW022142080726
473066UK00010B/705

* 9 7 8 1 0 0 9 5 7 0 0 4 6 *